Praise for *The Principal's*

"For over two decades, I have asserte[d] ... matter most are the ones that are a[uthored by those who have] effectively led schools or are curren~~tly leading~~ schools effectively. Why? Because they see the challenge and experience of leading schools through the lens of one who has lived the work. Jen Schwanke is that author. She knows the work because she lived it and performed it at a high level. She uniquely understands the complexities of managing conflict in schools on multiple levels because she not only lived it but understands the necessity for strategies that speak to it. I am excited about the prospects for this book, which I feel is an absolute must read for anyone in school leadership."

—**Principal Baruti Kafele**, education consultant, author, and retired principal

"Not all conflict is bad. Jen Schwanke helps principals understand the difference between productive conflict and negative, damaging conflict and gives them practical advice for how to facilitate the former while resolving the latter. Whenever you're working with human beings, some conflict is inevitable. But rather than avoid conflict, this book shows principals how to deal with it head on and keep it from derailing the important work they are doing in schools."

—**Robyn R. Jackson**, author of *Stop Leading, Start Building* and founder of Buildership University

"*The Principal's Guide to Conflict Management* is a practical, thoughtful, and honest response to the overwhelming demands school leaders face when managing conflict. In this book, Dr. Schwanke provides hard-learned lessons and useful applications you can immediately implement to navigate the journey. Chock-full of examples, stories, reflective practices, and useful scripts, this book is a must-read for school leaders. I can't wait to use it as a resource for my own work and to recommend it to every leader who wants help in managing conflict."

—**William D. Parker**, founder/CEO of Principal Matters, LLC

"In today's educational landscape, where conflict is inevitable, Schwanke reminds us to proactively embrace these conflicts with three simple but powerful words: anticipate, analyze, and act. This book is a reminder to all school leaders that when we create a culture that embraces productive conflict, it is healthier for the school community in the long game. A valuable read!"

—**Robyn R. Hamasaki**, former PK–8 Principal in Boulder, Colorado

THE
PRINCIPAL'S
GUIDE TO
CONFLICT
MANAGEMENT

Also by Jen Schwanke

The Teacher's Principal:
How School Leaders Can Support and Motivate Their Teachers

The Principal Reboot:
8 Ways to Revitalize Your School Leadership

You're the Principal! Now What?
Strategies and Solutions for New School Leaders

Teacher Observation and Feedback
(Quick Reference Guide for Leaders)

PATIENCE

JEN SCHWANKE

ELOQUENCE

CURIOSITY **THE** CONFIDENCE

PRINCIPAL'S

EMPATHY

GUIDE TO

ATTENTIVENESS

CONFLICT

CLARITY EQUANIMITY

MANAGEMENT

CHARACTER

ACCEPTANCE

ascd

Arlington, Virginia USA

2800 Shirlington Road, Suite 1001 • Arlington, VA 22206 USA
Phone: 800-933-2723 or 703-578-9600 • Fax: 703-575-5400
Website: www.ascd.org • Email: member@ascd.org
Author guidelines: www.ascd.org/write

Richard Culatta, *Executive Director*; Anthony Rebora, *Chief Content Officer*; Genny Ostertag, *Managing Director, Book Acquisitions & Editing*; Susan Hills, *Senior Acquisitions Editor*; Mary Beth Nielsen, *Director, Book Editing*; Megan Doyle, *Editor*; Thomas Lytle, *Creative Director*; Donald Ely, *Art Director*; Lisa Hill, *Graphic Designer*; Valerie Younkin, *Senior Production Designer*; Cynthia Stock, *Typesetter*; Kelly Marshall, *Production Manager*; Shajuan Martin, *E-Publishing Specialist*; Christopher Logan, *Senior Production Specialist*; Kathryn Oliver, *Creative Project Manager*

PAPERBACK ISBN: 978-1-4166-3273-3   ASCD product #124014
PDF E-BOOK ISBN: 978-1-4166-3274-0; see Books in Print for other formats.
Quantity discounts are available: email programteam@ascd.org or call 800-933-2723, ext. 5773, or 703-575-5773. For desk copies, go to www.ascd.org/deskcopy.

ASCD Member Book No. FY24-2 (Feb 2024 P). ASCD Member Books mail to Premium (P), Select (S), and Institutional Plus (I+) members on this schedule: Jan, PSI+; Feb, P; Apr, PSI+; May, P; Jul, PSI+; Aug, P; Sep, PSI+; Nov, PSI+; Dec, P. For current details on membership, see www.ascd.org/membership.

Library of Congress Cataloging-in-Publication Data

Names: Schwanke, Jen, author.
Title: The principal's guide to conflict management / Jen Schwanke.
Description: Arlington, Virginia : ASCD, 2024. | Includes bibliographical references and index.
Identifiers: LCCN 2023041687 (print) | LCCN 2023041688 (ebook) | ISBN 9781416632733 (paperback) | ISBN 9781416632740 (pdf)
Subjects: LCSH: School principals—Professional relationships—United States. | Conflict management—United States. | School personnel management—United States. | Educational leadership—United States.
Classification: LCC LB2831.92 .S393 2024 (print) | LCC LB2831.92 (ebook) | DDC 371.2/0120973—dc23/eng/20231017
LC record available at https://lccn.loc.gov/2023041687
LC ebook record available at https://lccn.loc.gov/2023041688

31 30 29 28 27 26 25 24 23   1 2 3 4 5 6 7 8 9 10 11 12

THE PRINCIPAL'S GUIDE TO CONFLICT MANAGEMENT

Acknowledgments

Thank you to Susan Hills, my acquisitions editor at ASCD, for the tremendous amount of time and energy you dedicate to my ideas and my writing. I am also grateful to Megan Doyle, Anthony Rebora, and Genny Ostertag at ASCD for giving voice to my work.

I am grateful to my superintendent, Dr. John Marschhausen, for his wealth of knowledge, ongoing mentorship, and endless support.

Gratitude also goes to the incredible teachers and leaders in Dublin City Schools, all of whom provide me with daily inspiration. The work of an educator is complex and ever-changing, and I love "being in the muck" with all of you!

As always, I am deeply appreciative of my husband, Jay, himself a masterful educator and leader, and my two children, Jack and Autumn. I feel tremendously lucky to have such a beautifully supportive and loving family.

Introduction

Managing conflict is an important skill for principals to develop, but rarely do principals receive specific training to prepare them for the conflict that might arise between parents, staff, and students. Many principals feel overwhelmed and underprepared as they address conflict, and it can begin to wear on them over time—especially if their efforts to alleviate or eliminate conflict fail.

Conflict does not always indicate a larger problem—it is simply the results of human beings working together. Many times, no intervention is needed at all. I recall one such conflict that occurred my third year of teaching. I found myself in a philosophical crossroads with the guidance counselor assigned to my teaching team. I'll call her Michelle. She was a well-respected, knowledgeable, and skilled professional, but I saw her as aggressive and domineering. I was the team leader, and she was our school's lead guidance counselor. We had a bit of an argument in front of our colleagues. Afterward, we were both angry, and for several days, there was a thick and impenetrable silence between us. I had no intention of backing down. I told the story wherever I could tell it, feeling pleased every time one of my colleagues commiserated with me—the counselor was bossy, they agreed, and taking liberties with her power. I was right. She was wrong. *Ha,* I thought.

One day after school, I was picking pencils up off the floor when my principal entered the room and closed the door.

"Listen," she said, "I spoke with Michelle today, and I know the two of you are not in a good place."

I felt a flash of anger. How dare Michelle tattle on me?

"What did she tell you?" I asked.

My principal, not one to suffer fools, got right to the point. "This has nothing to do with who said what to whom. I encourage you to work with Michelle to get through whatever issue has been created between the two of you. She is headstrong, but so are you. It is important that the two of you work as a team. If you don't, there will be a rift on this staff, and it will damage our school's mission. I recommend you set up a time to have coffee with her and talk it through." She stood to go. "And for the record, I have communicated the same message to her."

That evening, grading papers in my apartment, I thought through her suggestion. As much as I wanted to resist, my instinct reminded me that my principal was an experienced and visionary leader. She hadn't asked me to a meeting for her to mediate; she'd told me to figure it out. She'd said "recommend," but I knew it was stronger than a recommendation. I could ignore it . . . but I'd better not. The next day, I stopped in the guidance office and asked Michelle if she'd like to meet for coffee.

"I'd love that." She smiled.

We spent an hour in Starbucks after school. I worked to understand her perspective, and I could feel her working to understand mine. We arrived at a truce and agreed to put on a united front for the team and our colleagues. Our goal, we agreed, was to work together as a team. And that's just what we did—slowly, carefully, and with intentionality.

Over time, I developed a great deal of respect for Michelle and her work. I learned a tremendous amount from her, and she and I developed a powerful professional relationship. To this day, over twenty years later, even as she enjoys her retirement away from public education, we remain close. Had my principal not "recommended" a mature and timely response, I fear I would have missed out on a meaningful professional and personal friendship.

Unfortunately, not all conflicts are resolved this quickly or with such a positive outcome. On the contrary, some conflicts damage the collective efficacy of a staff, the effectiveness of a teacher, or the experience of a student. When left unresolved, it can fester and begin to affect the student experience. We see this most often with student-to-student conflicts, but even conflicts between a student and a teacher, or a teacher and a parent, can negatively affect the teaching, learning, and social environment for students. Unresolved conflicts can affect the climate and culture of a school for weeks, months, or even years. They manifest in emotions and feelings and are complicated by goals and actions that may not be in full alignment with others' goals and actions.

We would all love a conflict-free workplace, but it is fruitless to wish for one. Conflict is inevitable. For that reason, our goal should be to accept it, embrace it, and learn how to make it a healthy and productive part of what we do. We can do this by recognizing what mindsets and skills we will need to address conflicts and then following a three-step process to *anticipate, analyze, and act* upon them.

This book will help principals by providing insights, scenarios, tips, and strategies for leading through conflicts that arise in most school environments. Let's get started by taking a deeper look at some of the conflicts that arise in school and what can be done about them.

1

Conflict in Schools

I dislike conflict. As a child, fights with my siblings or arguments between my parents made me anxious and upset. Later, when I began working as a teacher and principal, any type of conflict—sometimes even the potential for it—would keep me up at night. I would imagine worst-case scenarios and visualize the darkest possible outcome. With time and experience, I have learned to manage conflict anxiety by using a calm, clinical, and process-driven mindset. Most important, I have learned to accept the inevitability of conflict—and even embrace it.

As educators, we are always attuned to the rise, fall, and impact of various types of conflict. Because everyone has, at one point, attended school in one educational setting or the other, they all feel they are the experts on schools—who does it well, what are the biggest problems, what changes should be made, and so on. There is no other public entity where literally every person has an experience to share, and they do so under the assumption that their experience is an accurate representation of everyone else's experience. Moreover, because any one of those people can take to social media to air complaints, their criticisms have, in recent years, eroded trust in teachers and schools, creating an environment in which educators have to build trusting connections with an increasingly dubious school or classroom community. Additionally, input from politically divisive legislators, legal challenges heard in courts, and a nonstop stream of stories in the media are fueling the flames, putting teachers and principals further on the defense against a seemingly endless stream of criticism and conflict. It often feels like a snowball barreling down a hill, gaining speed and impossible to stop.

Principals have a wide spectrum of approaches and responses to conflict. There are principals who fear it. They worry they cannot handle it—or feel they shouldn't have to—so they bury it, ignore it, or avoid it. Other principals respond by getting defensive, building a counterattack, or using their position of power to quelch it. But there are also principals on the other end of the spectrum. When they approach conflict, they remain confident and calm, navigating it without ever missing a stride. They consider their management of conflict to be an opportunity to build trust and respect from our stakeholders. They follow a process that ensures fair, honest, open communication, and they advocate for resolution that will improve school culture. In that sense, conflict management has enormous potential and possibility, because when it is handled well, it can maximize a principal's leadership impact and create schools built on empathy, kindness, and respect.

In other words, conflict is often seen as a negative experience, but it doesn't have to be. In fact, my hope is that, by using some of the strategies in this book, principals will move away from seeing conflict as a negative part of their job and toward embracing its inevitability and its potential.

Types of Conflict

To be human is to experience conflict—with ourselves, with others, and with the places in which we exist in the world. In a school environment, conflict is inevitable. It appears with regularity, sometimes as expected and sometimes without warning. Conflict can be silent and passive. It can be open, angry, and explosive. It can be ongoing, simmering conflict that does damage over time. It pops up between students, staff, parents, community, and any combination of these groups.

When it appears, principals are often looked upon to resolve, mediate, and eliminate it—not an easy task, especially these days. First, as explained above, many parents and community members feel like they are experts on education. They criticize teachers and administrators for perceived wrongs, creating layers of conflict that must be managed and resolved. Second, schools hold the responsibility of educating young people, each of whom comes with a set of loving, opinionated stakeholders—parents, family, friends, neighbors, teachers, and supporters—who want to advocate for the child. Finally, schools operate on the skills and talents of an entire staff of professionals, all with their own opinions and philosophies, varying work ethics, extensive background stories, and so on. Given all these factors, it is no wonder schools seem to have an endless serving of fresh conflict.

In my experience, there are two types of conflict: positive and productive or negative and damaging. The positive type has value for the school community and can be a sign of a healthy school culture. Healthy conflicts can lead to improvements in relationships, processes, and perspectives. It can mesh ideas together to create outcomes that have more impact; those outcomes, in turn, can enrich the experiences of staff, students, and families. On the first teaching team I worked, there were four of us, each with different backgrounds, training, and levels of experience. We were even generationally quite different. Yet, when conflict arose, it never threatened to harm our team dynamic, because trust and respect were firmly in place. The focus with which we listened to one another, the willingness to brainstorm solutions to problems, and the efforts we put into compromise and consensus were helpful and healthy. We certainly disagreed at times, but working through disagreements strengthened our team's dynamic.

When differing opinions are valued, considered, and folded into shared solutions, they can add a richness to the school's mission and purpose. It is a wonderful thing to experience a meeting or conversation in which someone can listen to one point of view and then safely and professionally provide an alternate viewpoint. Someone might say, "I actually disagree with that perspective, and I'd love to explain why." Or "I like that idea, and I think I can add something that might be even more effective." It's powerful, both as the giver and as the receiver of an alternate point of view, when conflicting opinions are a natural part of a problem-solving process.

Let's take a look at a few examples of common conflicts and how they might have a positive impact on a school.

Productive Conflict

Disagreements on Process

In schools, we often do things because we've always done them that way. When someone suggests an alternate approach, and others are willing to listen and consider the new idea, the conflict can inspire ideas and solutions that result in a better outcome. What starts as a disagreement can turn into a healthy and essential step to buiding a school community that is rich with diverse thoughts and viewpoints.

Opinions on a Student's Performance

Every student should feel successful at school. Relying on varying perspectives helps ensure each child has an advocate who sees their gifts. Teachers who have students struggling in their class might know of another teacher who has no problems with that student. Ideally, the first teacher might reach out to the second and say, "I am really struggling with a student and could use your help. Can you tell me what you did to have this student respond so well to your class?" Or "This student admires and respects you. I'd love for the three of us to sit down so I can observe your interactions with the student and learn how to connect the way you have." These varying experiences and opinions can merge to enhance a student's chance of success in all learning environments.

Teaching Philosophy

Not all educators—teachers or principals—share the same instructional philosophy. Just as there are variations in a teacher's purpose, priorities, and patterns, there are innumerable variations between teachers with what they hope to achieve in their teaching. Some will say they believe in building student confidence. Others are aiming for content mastery. Others want to expose students to the skills necessary for further independent exploration.

I can't help but think about two teachers at one of my previous schools. Both were masterful in the art of teaching, both were well loved and admired by students and colleagues, and both had consistently strong student data to support their approach to teaching—yet they had very different philosophies. One told me, "My goal is not to have my students memorize facts or formulas. I model kindness, patience, and perseverance, and I expect the same of my students. In that way, my teaching provides a learning environment where students can take risks and gain expertise at their own pace." The other teacher was very content driven. He worked tirelessly to have his students master mathematical formulas, equations, and algorithms because he was convinced that a deep understanding of math would help his students gain confidence in every other area of study they'd encounter.

Their philosophies were very different, but the outcome was the same: a positive learning experience for students and an eye on their future success. Varying philosophies have the potential to cause conflict, unless teachers accept that there is not one "winner" in instructional approaches. On the contrary, variety can be a way students experience diverse learning environments, which builds their skill to adapt and adjust to a similarly diverse world they will face in college and in their career.

Teaching Style

Similarly, teachers vary in their style and approach to teaching. Several years ago, I worked with two teachers who were teamed together, sharing a roster of students. One taught math and science; the other taught language arts and social studies. One of them valued a quiet, routine-rooted classroom. She never raised her voice, speaking only in soft, soothing tones; she kept lights low and the atmosphere calm; she avoided changes to her plans or spontaneous decision making. Next door, her teammate was a gregarious, loud, fun-loving jokester who would routinely abandon his original instructional plan, spontaneously deciding to present the day's concept in an unexpected and unique way. He loved finding "rabbit holes," as he called them—the chance to chase an idea down a different instructional path.

So different were their styles, it would be easy to assume the two couldn't possibly work well together. On the contrary, they were a beautiful pair, both accepting the differences of the other person and appreciating the value of having "an opposite." They even embraced it publicly. At the annual Back to School Open House event for parents and students, they showcased their differing classroom environments, although they took care to point out how both classrooms shared norms and expectations for behavior and academics. They believed their contrasting environments enriched the student experience and encouraged their students to adapt just as they would need to do in the real world. At the end of each year, in an effort to know how successful they'd been as an unconventional team, they asked students and parents to complete an exit survey indicating which approach the students and families preferred—a calm, quiet, predictable classroom or a less structured, unpredictable, and lively environment. Interestingly, year after year, the results were split almost exactly down the middle. Almost all respondents expressed that they appreciated the variations between the two classrooms.

Parent Input

When parents are concerned about their child's progress or achievement in school, their perspective can be a welcome addition to what we know about a student. Teachers and principals often toggle between wildly different parent expectations: sometimes parents are disengaged and never contact the school; other parents are heavily involved and want ongoing interactions with teachers. While working to engage the former group and set up healthy boundaries for the latter, teachers and principals can enhance school–parent partnerships by working toward mutually acceptable outcomes. I try to turn conflict with parents into a positive experience, using terms like *we* and *us* to demonstrate camaraderie and shared goals. With the right approach and mindset, disagreements with parents can lead to insights and ideas to better support the child.

Damaging Conflict

Unfortunately, it's not a certainty that conflict will result in a productive outcome. In fact, it's just as likely that a conflict will create ongoing negative friction. When conflict presents itself as a barrier to results, or when it becomes personal, it can damage relationships and trust for years. I know a teacher who hasn't spoken to one of his colleagues, beyond the perfunctory "hello" and "goodbye," for two decades. Unfortunately, this is not uncommon; we all know people who live with the long-term effects of a poorly handled conflict. When it escalates toward hurt feelings, blame, shame, resentment, accusations, or gossip, the aftermath of a conflict lingers for a very long time. Let's look again at the healthy outcomes listed above and see how the exact same conflict might, if managed poorly, cause long-term damage.

Disagreements on Process

If we've always done something a particular way, and a suggestion or idea is introduced to modify or modernize the approach, it can be met with resistance from those who fear change. If both sides dig in, it becomes a two-sided, unwinnable argument, forcing someone—usually the principal—to step in and choose one particular path. Unfortunately, that often means choosing between an old guard ("That's the way we've always done it; it works and we shouldn't change it") and a fresh perspective ("We need to evolve, and we have innovative ideas about how we can do it"). It's an impossible battle to win and can cast a negative shadow over the process of improvement and positive change.

Opinions on a Student's Performance

When one teacher struggles with a student and knows a previous teacher did not, the first teacher might assume the worst from the previous teacher. Years ago, a principal I know was approached by a teacher who was struggling to manage the escalating behaviors of one of her students, whom I'll call Weslyn. Since it was the first time Weslyn had ever exhibited aggressive or combative outbursts, the principal encouraged the teacher to reach out to Mr. P, Weslyn's previous teacher. She refused to do so, discounting his role in any previous successes. "I know Weslyn had no behavior problems in Mr. P's class, but that's because Mr. P just gives A grades to all students and doesn't challenge them to do anything. He was fine letting Weslyn just sit there and do nothing. In *my* class, she is actually required to do work, and she doesn't like it. I'm not going to ask Mr. P for help because I don't want his type of help." Unfortunately, the teacher also shared this perspective with her colleagues, and word traveled back to Mr. P. When he heard what the teacher was saying about him, trust was broken and never really restored.

Teaching Philosophy

Teachers watch, evaluate, and judge the philosophical approach of other teachers. Especially in an era of accountability, teachers can fall into a trap of competitive culture, judging themselves against the skill and expertise of their colleagues. They compare data on student growth and achievement. They watch which teachers are favored and which ones work the hardest. They see who follows expectations and who cuts corners. But environments driven by judgment are not healthy. If individual teachers have set attitudes and ideologies about their own work and refuse to accept the value of a different perspective, it becomes a never-ending tug-of-war game—who is a good teacher and who is not, who is there for the right reasons and who is there for the wrong ones.

Teaching Style

Similarly, when teachers assume their teaching style is the best and only way, conflict can arise with a colleague who has a vastly different way of teaching. The loud, fun, rowdy classroom against the quiet, ordered, structured one; the relaxed, laid-back teacher against the serious, goal-driven one. These dichotomies can create a negative divide if there is not a mindset of acceptance and universal value.

Parent Input

When parents raise questions or concerns about their child's learning experience, if teachers or administrators react in a negative, defensive way, it perpetuates the feeling that the teacher or school is wrong or has something to hide. Negative conflict festers when parents feel they must fight the school, shifting the relationship into a contentious one framed by the loss of trust.

Knowing about various types of conflicts still doesn't clear up *if* a principal should intervene, *when* they should do so, and *how* they should do it. Answering those questions requires a look at the role a principal has in helping others manage conflict.

The Role of the Principal

When people can't get along, is it the principal's job to intervene? It depends. We'll dive into that question throughout this book, because there are times the answer is an empathic "yes," such as when someone is a victim of bullying, aggression, or targeted abuse. There are also times a principal should intervene but should do so judiciously—perhaps from a distance or perhaps by supporting and empowering others to manage the conflict. And there are times when a principal should not intervene at all.

How do we know what path to take? The first step is to determine what *to intervene* means in any given situation. Intervention implies efforts to *fix, mediate,* or *resolve* conflict, but doing so can complicate the circumstances that created it in the first place. Besides, if principals tried to intervene in every conflict, they would never be able to keep up with the volume of issues—past, present, and future—that are guaranteed to pop up. *Managing* conflict, though, is something that is . . . well, manageable. It involves a process to *anticipate, analyze,* and *act* toward a positive outcome. Notably, the act part might not require actual action from the principal—instead, it might mean staying one step removed and empowering those who are involved to resolve it.

Early in my career, I was assistant to an excellent principal who deliberately did not step in when the conflict did not affect the work of the school. I was eager to be seen as effective, so I thought I needed to be everything to everyone. When a physical education teacher came to me to complain about the way her co-teacher took attendance, I listened carefully and then told her I'd get back to her with solutions. I went to my principal and recounted the whole story. "What should I do?" I asked.

He shrugged. "Nothing."

"Nothing?" I thought he must not have understood the urgency of the situation. "This is a big deal!"

"It is not. It is a silly disagreement. The two of them need to work it out," he said. "If she feels strongly enough that something needs to change, she will need to talk to her co-teacher herself. By coming to you, she's made it a bigger issue than it needs to be. She's essentially tattling and asking for you to take her side." He cautioned me against micromanaging—and getting into a spat about methods to take attendance would definitely be micromanaging. The better approach, he said, would be to encourage the teacher to talk to her teammate and work out a compromise—and if she wasn't willing to do so, she'd need to learn to live with the system the way it was. "No one is getting hurt, and there are no long-term consequences. In fact, no one is really even affected," he pointed out. He advised, "Know your role. Stay out of it." It took about 10 more situations just like this, with him mentoring me away from jumping in where I wasn't needed, before I truly understood the value in staying out of lower-stakes conflicts.

With time and experience, I can recognize that this wise principal was doing something beyond staying out of conflicts. He was also making it clear he would not intervene in disagreements that weren't critical, thereby establishing an expectation and culture in which teachers were empowered to work through minor issues on their own. This was especially applicable with some of the pettier complaints lodged from one person about another. He called them "ticky-tacky" conflicts— inconsequential, flimsy, and not worth considering. "Awww, that's just a ticky-tacky complaint," he would say. He knew that if we got involved in small things, well, then we would be asked to get involved in *other* ticky-tacky complaints and, worse, perpetuate a culture in which bothersome, annoying inconveniences were turned into big issues. When he heard about one of these types of conflicts, he would shrug and dismiss the problem from his consciousness. From him, I learned—and I offer this as a primary takeaway of this book—that many conflicts shouldn't even make it into the principal's awareness. They should be handled by those involved, or they should be given time so they can fizzle out. In other words, at times, the best course of action is no action. Principals can— and should be able to—count on others to work through small conflicts on their own.

Of course, some conflicts might need a principal to step in—namely, if they have potential to evolve into larger problems. It takes thought and care to decide when and how to intervene. In Chapter 4, we will specifically outline a process that will help principals decide if and how their input will be helpful. In the meantime, though, let's look at a few nuances of conflict and how they might affect the work of a school.

Conflict vs. Disagreement

Differing opinions, perspectives, experiences, and hoped-for outcomes create all sorts of disagreements. Disagreement isn't necessarily a precursor to conflict. A disagreement might be uncomfortable, but accepting it and embracing different opinions makes us better educators. Every day, teachers manage student disagreements. They instruct students to work through them during class, group work, or social situations. The same approach can be applied to adults, too, by accepting that a disagreement doesn't mean someone or something is wrong. It doesn't need to evolve into a conflict with bigger, long-lasting implications. It's just a difference of opinion, which is often a positive thing.

Conflict vs. Confrontation

In my experience, confrontations are to be avoided, because they are surprising and one-sided. They occur when a disagreement escalates into a conflict, is left unresolved by those best equipped to manage it, and then takes on an urgency in which at least one person thinks there should be a resolution—and it needs to happen *now*. Confrontations are the result of emotion and urgency. They cause drama, gossip, and anxiety, regardless of whether they occur with students or adults. Many people dread confrontation, because they dislike being surprised by someone who wants to power through a complicated problem in the heat of the moment.

Not many disagreements lead to confrontation, but when they do, it rarely goes well. We see this with students all the time—one student is pushed to the point of frustration or fury, and their heightened emotions explode into an argument or fight. The same is true for adults, although it occurs less often. The hope is that adults have the self-discipline and training to soften a potential confrontation into a calm, professional conversation.

Call Out vs. Call In

There is a key difference between calling someone out and calling them in. To call someone out is essentially a confrontation and implies you want them to know, publicly and emphatically, that they have done something wrong, and you intend to expose them. Calling someone *in* means you want to know more about their perspective while offering your own thoughts; you have the conversation quietly, privately, and with no discord.

When I hear someone struggling with conflict because they feel offended or hurt by someone else, I try to coach them toward a call-in. I ask, "Have you discussed your feelings with the other person? Do you feel you can both share your experiences and come to a common conclusion? What would be the appropriate setting to have a conversation? When might you feel ready to approach this in a calm and productive way?"

Outlier vs. Larger Problem

As a principal, I once had a student get in an altercation in the hallway. I'd known the student for five years, and she'd not so much as raised her voice to another student. Here, suddenly, she was kicking and screaming and fighting with a fierce intensity. Everyone involved, including the teacher who stopped the fight and brought her to the office, was surprised. We were all more interested in figuring out what had happened to trigger her anger rather than considering discipline, because her behavior had been so uncharacteristic. On the other hand, we often have students who are involved in altercations with peers with some regularity. The same is true with teachers and parents. If a teacher never escalates a conflict, but then something occurs that really bothers them, it's different from the teacher who has a daily complaint about something. If you go years without hearing from a particular parent, but then they reach out and want an immediate conversation, it's different from the parent who lodges complaints regularly. I don't approach these situations the same way, because an outlier will require different management than a repeated incident will. Outliers might be solved with conversation and support; frequent conflicts might involve more significant structural changes.

Flow

My superintendent talks about his goal in leadership: He wants all members of the staff to be in "flow." Flow happens when everyone knows their role, all opinions are valued, decisions are collaborative, and ongoing communication increases knowledge and buy-in. To achieve flow is to have a culture that works well without anxiety, competition, threats to territory, or unwelcome input. Students can find flow in a school, too, when they know the environment is calm and productive. Disagreement is part of flow, accepted and acknowledged without slowing the momentum of strong teaching and focused instruction. Disruptions to flow—confrontation, fights, disorganization, lack of shared goals—cause ongoing conflict and resentment.

Impact on Student Experience

As stated earlier, some conflict rises and falls without incident, and other conflict has potential for long-lasting damage. Knowing these things, one of the measures for how to manage it should be pointed toward the student experience. If the conflict has a negative impact on students or on the staff and community that serves students, it will need to be addressed. Why? Negative effects of conflict impede communication. It eliminates open, two-way dialogue, because people avoid or eliminate effective communication and thus create an environment in which people are misaligned. Ideally, with professional flow and with a productive communication culture in place, conflicts can actually improve the student experience.

Parent and Community Trust

For outsiders, watching, intervening, or hearing about conflict can feel exciting and dramatic—after all, it's what breaking news stories are made of. In a school setting, though, conflict should not be visible or affect the community. Years ago, my district was in local headlines for conflict between high-level district leadership, and the story dominated our community's conversation for several months. People talked about the conflict, not the good work of the schools. It took a long time to recover and shift the focus back to students, teachers, and the amazing growth happening every day. When conflict festers and communication breaks down, or if it permeates into a larger and much-discussed problem, it diminishes the positive things schools do and creates questions about trust and believability.

Culture and Climate

When a tiny pebble gets lodged in a shoe, it creates discomfort with every step taken. The same is true of conflict. One small conflict can fester into something painful and damaging to an entire school. There are many reasons why this happens. It might be teachers who simply cannot get along. It might be students who are constantly arguing, competing, or fighting. It might be a parent community that is intensely involved and does not have healthy boundaries to let the school function as it should. Finally, it might be attributed to principals who don't set the expectation of how to work through conflict in a healthy and productive way. Culture and climate can lead to positive results—or they can cast a pall on everything a school tries to do.

Modeling

Principals who effectively work through conflict are modeling for others how it can be done well. Unfortunately, I have known principals who do the opposite. They seem to thrive on the drama of conflict. They rush from one interpersonal crisis to another. They discuss it with others who are not involved, flaming the problem and increasing its reach. They take sides. They jump to conclusions and intervene with erroneous information. All of these missteps create a culture in which the school not only accepts constant conflict but also cannot function without it. Years ago, in my early years of teaching, I was in a school just like this. Teachers gossiped constantly about one another, their students, and their parent community; parents threw fits in an attempt to be heard; students created and fed drama. It was exhausting. And the principal was right in the middle of all of it. When I later moved and took a job in another part of the state, I spent the first six months wondering where all the drama was. It took me a long time to see that the principal's calm, professional modeling of conflict management permeated the mindsets of everyone in the school, so we had a school environment that was largely drama-free.

Support

A principal's involvement in conflict often comes down to various stakeholders vying for the principal's support. *Support* is a complicated concept, though, and it's worth considering what it means in the context of conflict management. Rather than supporting a particular side, I argue that support means the *principal is in favor of the conflict itself,* because rather than assume there is a right or wrong perspective, the principal can embrace the value of multiple perspectives.

In my favorite example of this, I once led a mascot review with a team of teachers in my school. The teachers on the committee came to the first meeting with very strong views. One side felt we should stick with our current mascot—a cardinal—because it was a long-standing symbol that was easily recognizable by students and families. The other side expressed their discomfort with the current mascot, pointing out the cardinal had been chosen as the mascot years ago because of an unsavory incident of equal parts horror and humor—a cardinal had apparently repeatedly crashed into a classroom window, over and over, until it fell to the ground, dead. Rather than choose one side, I proceeded as if each perspective were valued and worthy. In that way, I was able to support every person in the room. In time, we decided to leave the mascot alone, agreeing we would neither eliminate nor promote it; instead, we used a process to choose a school motto, which we actively promoted and utilized with the students. The cardinal faded away, but the motto remains in active use today.

Now that we've discussed some of the repercussions of conflict at school, let's think about how principals can know when to step in. Knowing that peaceful, productive resolution is not always possible, we'll talk about some strategies and solutions to ensure the good work of a school continues to flourish—in spite of the inevitable existence of conflict.

2

Complications of Conflict in Schools

Like most educators, I have a radar for conflict. When I was a teacher, I could scan a room and know if one of my students was feeling anxious or upset. I could speak with them and discover issues or concerns that were simmering beneath the surface. I learned which behaviors were concerning and how to communicate through them. Similarly, in my work as a principal, I can scan the faces looking at me during a staff meeting and know when there is something off—unease, disagreement, or discord, perhaps related to some of the content we're covering. I read faces, I read rooms, and I sense problems before I am told about them. This is what it means to be a teacher and leader.

We have all experienced relationships, both personal and professional, in which conflict rises and falls. It exists wherever humans exist, because humans are complex beings, as are our emotions and responses. Conflict can be a visible, tangible thing, loud and argumentative and full of emotion. It can also be silent, almost unidentifiable, nothing more than a feeling. Sometimes it disappears quietly, and other times it persists. For a principal, the challenge is to determine when to step in and do something about it or, as explained in the previous chapter, when to let it go and empower those involved to work through it.

To answer this, I've come up with a measure that works for me. I call it the Four Tens rule. It helps me overcome my instinct to jump in anytime I sense conflict. In fact, most times, what looks like a conflict might just be a bad mood, a bad moment, or a misunderstanding, and the best thing I can do is . . . nothing.

The premise behind the Four Tens rule is simple: just ask yourself, "Will this conflict matter in 10 minutes? Ten hours? Ten days? Ten years?"

- If a conflict will be forgotten in 10 minutes, it's not worth worrying about. Move on.

- Conflicts that will be bothersome in 10 hours—but not long beyond that—might be worth a short intervention, because these are the types of conflicts from which some learning is possible. These are the conflicts that might cause a problem between students at a lunch table, between staff members in a meeting, or between a parent and a teacher because of a brief misunderstanding. These conflicts can be resolved quickly with an acknowledgment, a clarification, or an apology, all of which allow everyone to move on easily. The conflict might be told as a story at someone's dinner table that night, but it can be an anecdote with a satisfactory ending.

- If the conflict will still be an issue in 10 days, it will need to be addressed, because 10 days is a long time for one or both parties to be upset. Besides, 10-day conflicts have the potential to grow into something more.

- If it will still be an issue in 10 years, it is usually because one or both parties has been deeply hurt, wronged, or treated poorly. Bullying behavior, personal insults, character diminishment, or attacks on someone's professional or personal belief systems can result in conflicts that last for years. Because these conflicts have long-ranging consequences, the intervention might need to be more significant, such as adjustments in structure and proximity.

The Four Tens rule helps me determine how and when I should intervene with a conflict. If I decide to step in, I consider the personality and perspective of the people having it, which helps me identify the root cause of the conflict. Doing so helps me decide how to approach the problem.

Let's back up a little. How can we get to the root cause of conflict? The most disruptive and damaging conflicts happen when someone is being cruel, aggressive, or deliberately damaging to another person. These are rare but have a big impact, requiring swift and thorough intervention. Fortunately, most conflicts are not as troublesome. They might be a result of communication that has gone awry or because of competing beliefs and approaches. They might be unintentional actions that lead to feelings of mistreatment or misunderstanding.

In a school setting, conflicts grow when there is a divide between how people approach their work, both in beliefs and in action. All people, young and old, tend to feel very strongly when they encounter philosophical differences. Many relationships have been tested and even broken because of variances in belief systems or because of misalignment of hoped-for outcomes. Let's take a look at some examples of how these differences manifest themselves into problems, starting with a difference in approaches to work.

Disparities in Work Ethic or Workload

A common recurring conflict between staff is a difference in commitment or work ethic. Consider, for example, a teacher intensely dedicated to their work. This teacher will stop at nothing to complete required tasks, and they take pride in doing their job well. Compare that teacher to one who looks to cut corners and decrease workload. The differences can cause problems of comparison because the teacher who considers themselves the harder worker can grow resentful when watching a colleague exerting what they perceive as minimal effort.

Of course, the teacher who cuts corners isn't necessarily doing anything wrong. Cutting corners might mean an efficient and "work smart" approach. I can use myself as a negative example here. I have always been the type of person who measures myself by how hard I work, and I used to get quite upset when I felt others were not matching my efforts. This is foolish in many ways, not least because I often work myself to a place of being exhausted. When I'm tired, I compare myself to others. If

I perceive others aren't dedicating enough hours and effort, I begin to resent them.

It's also foolish because I work hard but don't always work smart. I have watched colleagues who work *very* smart, and I admire their efficiency and output while they maintain equilibrium. One of my work-smart colleagues once asked why in the world I am so *intense* all the time. "You should learn to cut back on hours, be more efficient, and let some things go," she said kindly. "In other words, just . . . chill out." Her real talk honestly made me laugh, but I tried to take her words to heart. Fortunately, I have never experienced open conflict in my approach to work, although I am sure plenty of people are annoyed by it. The healthiest thing I can do—and the way I avoid conflict—is accept others' approach to work and refuse to let it become a point of contention. As a leader, I can model and communicate my belief that differences in work ethic are acceptable and even welcomed. After all, it is to be expected that professional teams are not made up of a perfect balance of time, effort, expertise, and dedication. Embracing these differences, and refusing to judge the work of others, adds a great deal of value to what we do.

What if that doesn't happen, though? Effort disparities do turn into larger conflicts if one person is clearly and consistently carrying the workload of others. For example, a principal friend of mine recently called to ask what I would do if a team of two teachers were stuck in an apparent stalemate of internal conflict. One of the teachers, whom we'll call Ms. B, contributed very little to the work of the team. She planned her instruction and taught her students well, but the other teacher, Mr. N, seemed to work twice as hard, taking on a massive amount of residual work for the two of them. He dove into project-based learning units, planned field trips, arranged all the parent–teacher conference schedules, managed student discipline, and so on. Usually happy to be the hardest-working person in the room, he had begun to grow frustrated that Ms. B sat back and let him take on many of the most complex tasks. These things were important to him, as he felt they contributed to an excellent student experience. But Ms. B didn't feel that all the extras were necessary and thought Mr. N went way overboard. On her part, she was resentful, too, feeling Mr. N pressured her to be involved in projects and experiences she felt were outside her responsibilities. Like any relationship, their dynamic had become interwoven with their teaching identities, and they were irritated with one another without ever having really talked about it. Mr. N's efforts enabled Ms. B to give a minimum amount of effort; Ms. B's perceived disengagement forced Mr. N to keep the team afloat, both in operation and in reputation.

When my friend asked for guidance, I told her I thought this was something Mr. N needed to discuss with Ms. B. They would need to decide what they were committed to keeping, what they could let go, and how the two could work together more peacefully. Of course, Mr. N would need to release some control and trust that a different way was perfectly acceptable; at the same time, Ms. B needed to be willing to take on more work to meet their shared goals.

It wasn't an easy problem to solve, because Ms. B was not actually doing anything wrong. Dynamics like this are just a complicated type of competition—who works harder, who is more committed, who is "better"—but such competitions are unproductive because there are no winners and certainly no prize. Indeed, workload disparities in education have deep roots. The system is built on "equal pay for equal work," so most teachers follow a fixed, predictable salary rate. A Brookings Institute study of teacher pay outlined the benefits to a system that provides equal wages, especially because it lessens evidence of pay inequity based on race, ethnicity, gender, or education level. Yet it also normalizes inequities in credentials, accountability, student progress, and required work responsibilities (Hansen & Quintero, 2022). When teachers have a benefit package of accruing sick days, for example, conflicts can arise with how this benefit is viewed. I recently spoke with a teacher who's lived with a low-grade frustration for years because of this. She misses just one or two days of school a year, while a teacher across the hall calls off sick at least 20 times a year, sometimes many more. The teacher feels like sick days should only be used if very ill; her colleague considers sick days as an earned benefit that should be used up. The different viewpoints cause friction—mostly on the side of the person who took a conservative view on the use of sick days. This is just one small example of the way work philosophy and competition can cause conflict in schools.

Let's dive into another example. As we know, the amount of work and effort required to be an effective teacher has no standardized measuring system. It's not for lack of trying; for years, efforts have been made to hold teachers accountable to their professional preparedness and output, both at the licensure renewal level and at the student achievement level. If anything, these efforts have only increased the disparity between teachers who compare the expectations placed upon them with teachers who do not have the same expectations. Of course, the viewpoint of each person is dependent on their perspective. A teacher of high-level math or science—say, an International Baccalaureate chemistry teacher—makes the same amount of money, has the same assigned work hours, has the same benefits package, and retires at the same time as a middle school physical education teacher. The chemistry teacher might argue her content is difficult, the expectations fierce, the accountability intense, the outcome impactful. She might also argue that student mastery can either enhance or diminish college and career choices and thus a student's entire adult future. The physical education teacher might argue that learning about health, movement, and physical skill is an essential competency with lifelong implications. Effective instructional methodology requires planning, flexibility, and relationship rapport to create enthusiasm and engagement for all students, especially those who are reluctant or resistant to participate. All students take P.E., while only motivated, focused, science-loving students would take an advanced chemistry class. Both of these arguments are accurate, of course, but the belief that one teacher has a more intense workload with higher stakes attached to it is something that will never truly be settled.

Over the years, I've heard hundreds, maybe thousands, of complaints about disparate workloads. All principals have. There is very little that can be done about it, especially in an industry that negotiates for equal pay, equal evaluation systems, and equal benefits. One common retort to a teacher complaining about workload inequality is something along the lines of "Well, you can always add a certification to your license and teach something else"—a response that is not helpful and rarely welcomed.

Most teachers understand and accept that there are positive and negative aspects to their teaching assignment, and they appreciate the positive outcomes of a standardized salary and work schedule. Still, these perceived imbalances create conflicts—sometimes open ones, sometimes beneath the surface. I have come to accept this inevitability, but I actively work to counter any negative effects on my school's collective efficacy. I try to create a culture in which every person is valued for the role they have. Educating the whole child takes a well-rounded staff, and we couldn't do it well unless all content areas are represented. Arts, science, humanities, and student electives all have an important role in a complete education.

Disparate workloads are not just an adult problem. Any student who has worked on a group project has probably felt an imbalance in effort and commitment, leading to frustration about unequal workloads. In fact, many students struggle with group projects. My niece is a student who hates group work. When she talks about it, she gets visibly agitated and angry. I once tried to explain why teachers love group work. "It is part of learning to collaborate, share ideas, and improve the final product of the assignment," I told her. She rolled her eyes. "Yeah, yeah. That's what they say. But it just means I do all the work and everyone else sits there." She felt her grade would lower if she didn't go above expectations to provide an excellent product. She knew she could do less, but she didn't want to accept a lower grade. When I asked her if her teachers tried to monitor the effort put into a particular assignment, she said, "Well, sure. They try. But I have to get along with these other kids, so I'm not going to tell the teacher they didn't do anything. When teachers ask, we all say the work was equal, and then we all get the same grade and everyone is happy. Except me."

Disparate workloads cause a buildup of frustration. It's a slow burn. Principals and teachers are usually aware of the reality of these imbalances between students, but often there is not an obvious solution to them. Saying, "Well, life's not fair!" is a true statement but not necessarily a comforting one. When students are struggling with workload disparity, helping them clearly outline responsibilities for each group member and then providing feedback and point value to each specific role will reduce the probability of conflict.

Personality Differences

In addition to workload conflicts, another frequent precursor to conflict can be attributed to differences in personality and style. In Chapter 1, we discussed some of these differences and how they lead to conflict. We see this often in students. Although adults are generally more adept at knowing and recognizing when someone approaches the work—and the world—with a different lens, young people are not as experienced in accepting different personalities. Introverts and extroverts. Leaders and followers. Creators and consumers. Teammates and loners. Planners and reactors. I have a dear friend who has worked for almost 20 years with a teacher whose personality is the complete opposite of hers. The first few years they worked together were very rough. My friend, who craves camaraderie and teamwork, struggled to accept how much her colleague liked to work alone. My friend went through stages—resentment, anger, frustration, loneliness, and then, finally, acceptance. She recognized she would not, and would never, get the type of relationship from her colleague that she craved, and in that recognition, she was able to let it go. She found professional camaraderie with teachers at a different grade level and has settled into a peaceful and mutually respectful relationship with her teammate.

There are many more examples of common precursors to conflict because of personality and style. Let's take a look at some of the character traits that might cause conflict with others.

The Competitor

It's natural to feel a sense of competition to win an outcome—to have things turn out the way we'd like. As explained earlier, this often happens among teams of teachers. An idea is born, and in the process of working through steps to achieve the shared desired outcome, colleagues turn on one another to have *their* vision be the one everyone follows.

The Authoritarian

There are people who take over and don't accept the input of others. I once worked with a teacher, whom I'll call Ms. S, who was such a strong and confident leader she couldn't seem to allow others to do anything. In one example, someone on her grade-level team proposed an idea for a field trip. It was an exciting opportunity, tying beautifully into an extensive project the students had been working on. But after the idea was proposed and decided, Ms. S essentially took over. She called a meeting and reviewed the work that needed to be done then assigned tasks to each person—securing tickets, collecting permission slips and medical forms, managing funds, sending requests for bus transportation. Everyone set out to work. But Ms. S kept stepping in and redoing tasks that weren't completed to her satisfaction. Every single detail was overseen and scrutinized by Ms. S. The other teachers felt belittled and disrespected, so they banded together in pulling back from offering their help. When there were snags on the trip—as should be expected—the rest of the teachers crossed their arms and shrugged, letting Ms. S take the blame and manage the response.

The Defender

When people have an instinct or inclination to be defensive, conflict can arise when another person offers a differing opinion, additional input, or constructive criticism. Defensive people are quick to explain why they aren't culpable for the way things turn out. "It's not my fault," they say, or, "I wouldn't have done it that way, so don't look to me for explanations or solutions."

The Blamer

"It wasn't me," says the person looking to assign a problem to someone else. This happens all the time, most often with students but also with many adults. Think how many times an incident occurred and you asked students to explain their role. "She started it," they might say, or, "It was his idea." There are countless phrases used by blamers: "Not me." "I wouldn't know anything about it." "It wasn't my idea."

The Insecure

When we don't feel good about ourselves, it is easy to judge or find fault with others, especially those who seem to have everything figured out. A friend of mine is a principal at an elementary school. Her children attend her school. Each summer, when making student–teacher assignments, she places her children carefully, knowing the statement it makes when a teacher has the principal's child on their roster. One year, she placed her son in a class of a teacher who was known to be excellent. The other teacher in the grade level, whom we'll call Miss L, was an excellent teacher too—but she was also very sensitive and anxious, so the principal thought having her son in the class would be a challenge for Miss L. Instead, *not* having the principal's son in class seemed to trigger all Miss L's insecurities. She was resentful of her colleague, she questioned whether the principal liked her, and she gossiped to other colleagues about the principal having favorites.

The Sufferer

I once worked with a principal who was at an impasse with two staff members, both of whom frequently came to him to complain about one another. One was a special education intervention specialist, and the other was an 8th grade history teacher. They worked together in an inclusion-model classroom for one class period a day. It was 45 minutes of daily stress for them both. Each felt the other had fewer job responsibilities, less pressure, and a philosophy that was less noble. "They each feel the other has it better, and each feels some drive to prove their job is harder," the principal said. They were stuck in what I call a suffering contest, both looking for external validation that they, in fact, were "suffering" more than the other.

The Anxious

When we feel anxious about an outcome, it may make us feel that we are not in control. In seeking to get some control, we worry, considering all possible repercussions to a situation. As explained earlier, I get very anxious—about conflict, about work that needs to be done, about who is going to do it. When others don't share my propensity for worrying, I can feel very alone and very resentful. But left unacknowledged or ignored, resentment can be a direct pipeline to conflict.

The Angry

I recently traveled out of state for a school visit. I arrived just as students were being dismissed to the gym for an assembly. As the students passed in a thick, loud throng, I rested against a wall in the hallway. I was standing next to a teacher I didn't know, so I introduced myself. I was taken aback to discover he was furious. He hated the disorganized, haphazard way students were dismissed to go to the office. He felt it led to pushing, shoving, and anxiety for the students as they rushed to find seats. "Every time the principal gets on the intercom and dismisses all 800 students to the gym, I feel my blood pressure rise. I stand here and get more and more angry. The principal won't listen to my ideas about fixing the problem. He thinks I'm making a mountain out of a molehill," the teacher said. He'd thought about solutions, he said, but they fell on deaf ears. I recognized an unfortunate cycle: He was presenting himself as so angry that his principal likely avoided seeking his input, which in turn increased his anger—creating ongoing conflict between him and his administrator.

How to Respond

Recognizing some of these disparities and personalities and characteristics is the first step to accepting the inevitability of conflict and knowing how to respond. In Chapter 4, we will outline a process to address conflict by following an *anticipate-analyze-act* cycle. Before we get there, though, I have a few tricks I've learned over the years that help me manage problems that arise as a result of conflict.

Avoid HALTS in Ourselves and Others

Looking inward to evaluate one's physical or emotional state is a skill explicitly taught to those in recovery programs to overcome an addiction, but it is applicable in any conflict situation. The trick is to look to see if you are *hungry, angry, lonely, tired, or stressed* before making decisions or responding with an unclear mind. Taking this physical and emotional inventory helps avoid situations in which emotion overrules rationality. There are two parts to this. The skill to avoid HALTS is important in oneself—say, the principal, who shouldn't make any decisions or intervene with problems when feeling this way—but it's also important that we know if others are feeling HALTS. Ironically, educators tend to know this about students. When a student is escalated or upset, we ask if they need water, food, a break, rest, a friend, or a conversation—yet we won't always do the same for ourselves or our adult colleagues.

The Value of Listening—Really Listening

People don't always say what they mean. In fact, sometimes words they use cloak their intended meaning. In one of my frequent presentations to principals, I go through a list of phrases that are commonly said to principals, and we consider what people *really* mean when they say these things. We will go into many more in the final chapter, but one example is when teachers criticize a process by saying, "That's not what I was told." This usually means they feel taken aback by new information or don't feel confident in implementing a new idea. When a parent says, "My child would never lie," usually they are feeling shocked or uncertain about something their child has said or done. There are many other examples, but the important thing to remember is this: When we listen with patience, compassion, and careful questioning, we can reveal much more than what words are said. The skill of listening makes all the difference in understanding how people feel when they are involved in conflict.

Respond Without a Qualifier

Something true and profound we should all know: In compound sentences connected by a *but,* the first half of the sentence doesn't really matter. I constantly remind myself that using *but* disqualifies what comes before it. Think about someone saying, "I like your hair, but your outfit doesn't really work." Hearing this, we don't remember that our hair looks great; we just rush to change the outfit. Similarly, when we work through a conflict, saying something helpful or understanding and then following it up with "but . . ." leads the listener to forget the positive thing and focus on whatever came after the *but*. Educators use *but* all the time when talking to parents. It comes from the "positive sandwich" approach many of us learned early in our training: say something nice, say something difficult, and then say another nice thing. I would argue we can say nice things without making it sound like they're irrelevant to the conversation. Instead of "Your son is a great kid, but he isn't completing his assignments," we can say, "Your son is a great kid. I'm really enjoying his personality, his quick wit, and his ability to make any situation a little lighter." Pause. Wait. Listen to anything the parent has to say. Then, in a separate sentence, "In class, we are working on his ability to see an assignment through to completion."

Later in this book, I'll discuss a situation in which a student, who was working to overcome the manifestations of her autism, grew very upset with her teacher. She had thrown her supplies and materials across the room. I was called to help deescalate the situation, but when I arrived, the teacher had already helped the student become calm. They were talking through what had happened. I listened as the teacher quickly took responsibility for her part in the situation. "I know you were frustrated, and part of it is my fault for not recognizing you needed more time to finish your work. I am so sorry for the role I played in this." I waited for her to say, "But you cannot throw things or put others in danger." She didn't. She simply ended her sentence with her apology. The student thought for a moment before nodding and then acknowledging that throwing things was a poor response. Together, the two reviewed alternative options for the future. The situation reminded me how helpful it is when we resist a *but,* because it often allows for more productive and two-sided conversations.

Avoid Email

Conflict resolution belongs in conversation, not email. We all know how email fails to adequately capture intent, emotion, and nuance. We also know the complications email brings. I once received an email from a parent who was asking me to mediate between her and another parent. The email was long but exceedingly articulate. One by one, she outlined perceived slights from the other parent, dating back months, and out-lined ways their conflict was affecting their children. Because it was so well written and carefully documented, I assumed the parent's per-spective was accurate. Fortunately, I followed my rule of not mediating between parents, and the issue did not become my problem; however, later, I learned how wrong my assumptions had been. Most of her claims were inaccurate and could even have been considered slanderous. The parent's email created bias—in me—simply by the skillful way it was written. I have been a victim of this when emails are well written and have also done it on the other side; if an email is riddled with grammar and mechanical errors, if it is disorganized and difficult to follow, I might dismiss it prematurely and unfairly. There are other problems with email as a conduit for conflict:

- You never know who actually wrote the email.
- Protected by their keyboards, people say things on email they won't say in person.
- The complainant might be using email to document an investigation and catch any missteps.
- In states and schools subject to public records laws, all emails are public records and thus can be pulled anytime by anyone.

For that reason, I prefer having real-life conversations, either on the phone or in person. The exception, which we will address in Chapter 7, is when you *do* want an official record of the conversation, perhaps when dealing with a highly volatile or litigious situation.

Document

Shared documents can be a valuable instrument for managing con-flict. This is a big difference between email—which, as stated earlier, might be best to avoid—and sharing documentation of agreed-upon next steps. Email is a one-sided communication, with all the complications that come with cc, bcc, forwards, editing, and deletions. Shared docu-ments outline a clear and established path forward. When in a group to discuss a problem, I will often create a document on a screen and then immediately share it with others—while they are sitting there—so they can edit, add, or review at their convenience. When we agree on key details, I'll document them—what needs to happen next, what timeline should be followed, what action steps will be completed, and who is involved. I do this with students, teachers, and parents. When all input is added, the document can be shifted to viewer mode to preserve and document what was discussed and decided. It also serves as a starting point if needed later. As an example, if a principal has intervened with one particular teacher multiple times and eventually decides to move in the direction of a formal improvement plan, previous documentation—which, again, was fully transparent and visible—provides the bricks on which the plan will be built. It will include dates, stakeholders, those who have been affected, and desired outcomes. The same applies to ongoing student conflicts. Putting things in writing for students, even very young students, makes action steps and plans more tangible.

These strategies will help you navigate some of the complications that arise when people are in conflict with one another. Because conflicts are often the result of disparities in workload, philosophy, and personality type, managing them requires skill, empathy, expertise, and wisdom. Developing such professional traits, and learning how to foster them in others, will be the focus of the next chapter.

3

Mindset Skills for Successful Conflict Management

To successfully facilitate or mediate a conflict, principals benefit from developing certain interpersonal skills and professional mindsets. Although many have not been expressly trained in the acquisition and refinement of soft skills, they certainly learn them—both from their early-career time as a teacher and from on-the-job training as a principal. These skills mold the way we think—our mindsets—and then create habits. The more they are revisited and utilized, the more they become part of what we do and how we do it. In this chapter, we will look at a few of these mindsets and consider how principals can embed them in their practice.

After each one, you will see a short reflection consisting of statements that might indicate whether a particular mindset skill is a strength for you. You might use these reflection statements after a specific event, or you might consider them related to your overall leadership style. You may choose to reflect on these questions on your own or think about them with a trusted professional friend—someone who will give you honest and helpful feedback. Personally, I like to draw on a combination of both; I like to engage in continual revisitation of my mindset skills, but I also benefit from asking a close colleague how aligned my mindset is with successful leadership. There is growth opportunity in both approaches.

Patience

To get us started, let's talk about patience (see Reflection 3.1). Leading with a patient mindset is a particularly challenging task in school leadership. The job is exceedingly fast paced. It demands quick thinking and rewards decisiveness. I have always struggled to be patient because, like many principals, it isn't something that comes naturally to me. I like things to move quickly toward a clear, solid resolution to a problem. Driven by checklists, I thrive on efficient completion of tasks. But managing conflict is not an exercise in speed. It is better to slow the pace and give time for clear thinking and thoughtful planning. Particularly when the conflict is causing pain for others, time is a salve for hurt feelings, mistaken meaning, and problematic responses. Additionally, a patient mindset gives time for an issue to resolve in a natural way. In attempting to be fixers, principals sometimes unintentionally step in to try to solve problems that would dissipate on their own, making patience a gift in alleviating the stress of overextending one's reach in conflict management.

Reminding myself to be patient has become a regular part of how I continue to improve. I often self-reflect—particularly after a specific incident of conflict management—by asking myself if my mindset was aligned with the descriptors in the "strong mindset" column or whether I have some room to grow.

Reflection 3.1 Patience Reflection

Patience

A Strong Mindset:	Room for Growth:
• You give yourself time to think. • You do not rush toward solutions. • When you find yourself feeling rushed, you discipline yourself to pause, breathe, and take a step back.	• Everything feels like an emergency. • Your anxiety is transferred to others. • You work fast; slow processes are frustrating to you. • You'd rather do something quickly—and know it is complete—than pause and wait.

Questions for Reflection:
- Do you feel like you're always responding to crisis, or are you able to calm your mind before reacting?
- Do you follow a systematic process when responding to conflict, or do you just take problems as they come?
- Are you often going back to clean up impulsive responses and decisions, or do you generally slow down and get your response right the first time?

Poise

With patience as an anchor, let's think about a few other mindsets that serve principals well, starting with poise (see Reflection 3.2). I always admire people who present themselves as calm, balanced, and in control. A friend of mine, whom I'll call Sherri, is a superintendent in a neighboring district and does this beautifully. She possesses elegance and grace in her behaviors, movements, and thought patterns, making her my role model in conflict management. No matter the situation, she exudes quiet confidence. I've seen her handle everything from a minor disagreement between staff members to a contentious public challenge with the same demeanor. It's like she is always on camera, projecting her best self to a wide media audience. I once asked her how she does it. "Nature and nurture," she said, smiling. She explained that it is a combination of her personality and concerted effort. She is a naturally tranquil person, she said, but she also focuses on maintaining her poise in difficult situations.

Reflection 3.2 Poise Reflection

Poise	
A Strong Mindset:	**Room for Growth:**
• You remain calm in chaotic situations. • Others are drawn to your sense of equilibrium. • When challenged, you remain thoughtful and in control. • Your presence in a room naturally calms others; they don't feel rushed or anxious when near you.	• You freeze or flounder during a crisis. • You don't make strong decisions when under pressure. • You are paralyzed by the strain of getting everything right. • Drama, anxiety, or uncertainty surrounds you during difficult times, amping up these feelings in others.
Questions for Reflection: • Do others tend to keep their distance, or do they come to you for guidance and direction? • When challenges occur, do they cause you to react in ways you later regret, or do you handle them with composure and control?	

Eloquence

One of the strategies leading to Sherri's poised appearance is her eloquence (see Reflection 3.3). Like patience, this is a challenge for me, as I sometimes chatter too much when trying to find the right way to communicate in a conflict situation. Sherri, on the other hand, will pause and think until she finds the words or phrases that will capture her intended message. We were together in a meeting once in which a group of teachers was frustrated about a reduction in staff. I tried to explain the reasoning—a necessity based on class sizes and finances—but found myself stumbling over a lot of jargon about enrollment, projections, funding sources, and future operations costs. I wasn't answering their questions. Sherri touched my arm to quiet me and said to the teachers, "I understand how difficult this is to hear, but the truth is simple. We do not need these positions, as student-to-teacher ratios are well below our district's norm. We are re-allocating them to save money." That was it. When the teachers had additional questions, she provided a consolidated review of data and numbers to reinforce her point. She said exactly what I'd been trying to say, using one-tenth of the words. Each was chosen with care so she could offer a simple, honest, and on-point explanation for a complicated situation.

Reflection 3.3 Eloquence Reflection

Eloquence	
A Strong Mindset:	**Room for Growth:**
• You don't speak unless you have something to say. • You read your audience, adjusting your communication to fit their needs. • You think before you speak. • Others listen when you talk.	• After conversations with you, others often have additional questions about the things you've already explained. • You tend to try to fill silence with chatter, often losing your intended message along the way.

Questions for Reflection:
- When leading conversations, do you formulate your thoughts first, or do you tend to process them out loud? If it's the latter, do others think you're talking too much, or do you let others know you're processing ideas and would like their input?
- Are you uncomfortable with silent times in conversation, or do you recognize it as a space to think and prepare?

Curiosity

Taking care with words extends to how we ask questions, why we ask questions, and what solutions might be available. In analyzing conflict—the first step to a process we will discuss in Chapter 4—we are more effective if we approach our investigation with curiosity (see Reflection

3.4). A fixed mindset is one in which we try to catch the person to blame for conflict and provide consequences. When someone gets in trouble, it feels simpler: identify the villain and protect the victim. But moving away from a fixed mindset and instead approaching conflict with curiosity is an extremely effective way to fully understand and respond.

In college, I minored in psychology because I found human behavior to be a fascinating area of study. I still do. I am curious about why people act, think, and speak as they do, and I like to think of disagreements as a mystery to be solved. *What happened? Why did it happen? What were the intentions of those who are involved? What were their intended outcomes? What could have been done differently?* Finding all the details—the historical events that led to the current situation, the actions and words that have been used, the different hoped-for outcomes of everyone involved—happens more easily when we approach the search with a curious heart and mind rather than simply trying to decide who is right or wrong.

Solutions can also be considered with this mindset. You might wonder, *What can be done to improve the situation? How can we avoid a repeat? What will make everyone feel safe, valued, and seen? What structures or systems are holding us back?*

Reflection 3.4 Curiosity Reflection

Curiosity	
A Strong Mindset: • You know you don't know what you don't know. • You see every situation as a new one. • You avoid making assumptions based on the first information you get.	**Room for Growth:** • You jump to conclusions. • You often find yourself having to change your original response plan based on new information. • You think you know the end of the story before hearing all the details.
Questions for Reflection: • Do you tend to jump to conclusions and solutions, or do you take time to gather details and make a thoughtful plan? • Are you prone to making erroneous assumptions, or can you catch yourself and have the discipline to slow down and get the facts?	

Confidence

When we don't approach conflict management with curiosity, we are making an assumption that we already know and understand all the nuances and possible solutions—which is unlikely to be true. This leads to our next mindset (see Reflection 3.5). Being curious helps us have confidence as conflict managers. If we approach disagreements as though we already know everything—which *looks* a lot like confidence—we'll often be wrong, and these errors actually erode confidence. We've all made unintentional but significant mistakes by making bad assumptions. These mistakes create insecurity and doubt—especially when our errors lead to false accusations or unfair discipline. That's why leading with confidence shouldn't exist in the space of confidence in *information;* it should be confidence in *process.* Rather than saying, "I know exactly what happened and how to handle this," we should find our confidence in knowing we will be fair, thorough, and supportive: *I know how to anticipate potential conflict, analyze applicable details, and act in a way that honors the people involved. I know I will do it with patience, poise, care, and curiosity.* A process-rooted confidence can be applied in any situation and almost guarantees a higher success rate than jumping to quick conclusions or making assumptions.

Reflection 3.5 Confidence Reflection

Confidence	
A Strong Mindset:	**Room for Growth:**
• You have faith in yourself. • You know your best is good enough. • You use feedback to elicit change. • You follow a process of anticipate-analyze-act. • You don't let your "gut" be your decision-maker.	• You live with constant self-criticism and insecurity. • You question yourself even as you are in the act of leading. • Feedback makes you question your abilities. • Your fear of messing up overrides your decision-making process.
Questions for Reflection: • Do you tend to doubt yourself, or do you believe in your own efficacy? • When you receive feedback, do you criticize yourself for missteps, or do you think about ways to grow from the information? • Do you make decisions based on fear or anxiety, or do you deliberate toward thoughtful decisions?	

Empathy

Following a fair and open-minded process helps us lead with empathy (see Reflection 3.6). On the evening I write this, I am reflecting on a parent meeting I had earlier in the day. I was in the meeting to help a teacher provide the rationale for why a particular approach to reading instruction had been selected for this parent's child. The parent threw out questions in rapid-fire form, and the teacher could barely answer one before the parent would interrupt to ask another question. I could see the teacher had begun to question her decisions; she looked anxious and shaken. I could also see the parent's frustration elevating. I felt bad for both, because I knew each had the best of intentions for the child.

I stepped in. "There isn't a teacher in the universe who gets up in the morning and hopes to fail in teaching students to read," I said gently. "Especially this teacher." The teacher looked at me gratefully. Then, I said, "There isn't a parent in the universe who wakes up and says, 'I'd like to get in an upsetting argument with my child's teacher today.'" The parent smiled and nodded. "I'm concerned this is becoming a meeting about who is right and who is wrong, which is not why we're here. Let's talk about the plan for helping the student and what concerns we each have about that plan." The temperature in the room softened, and both were able to communicate more clearly under the safe knowledge they both were trying to help the child. Managing conflict by having empathy for everyone, and by stepping in to remind participants of positive intentions, can sometimes dissipate a potentially contentious situation.

Reflection 3.6 Empathy Reflection

Empathy	
A Strong Mindset: • You understand that everyone is in the midst of a complicated journey. • You can transfer your own experiences to various situations. • You can identify when someone is feeling insecure, angry, or frustrated.	**Room for Growth:** • It's difficult for you to imagine how others are feeling. • Your own experiences overshadow your ability to connect with others. • You pick a side and stick with it, regardless of the point of view of those not on that side.
Questions for Reflection: • Do you struggle to put yourself in the mindset of someone else, or can you readily imagine how they are thinking and feeling? • Do you dismiss others without considering their perspective, or can you analyze a situation and recognize the complications related to it?	

Trust

Empathy does more than just soften sharp edges. It also builds trust (see Reflection 3.7). As a principal, putting yourself in the heart and mind of others works wonders. Most people want to be seen as someone with positive intentions who, when in a conflict, will work toward a solution. If a student, teacher, or parent knows the principal will listen without judgment or preconceived notions, they will trust them to intervene, manage, and resolve conflicts. Trust is further reinforced by a principal who follows through on promises, outlines workable plans, and creates a sense of collaboration with others. It removes contentiousness and replaces it with a calm belief that everything will work out.

Reflection 3.7 Trust Reflection

Trust	
A Strong Mindset:	**Room for Growth:**
• Others confide in you when they are feeling vulnerable.	• Others do not feel comfortable confiding in you.
• You listen without judgment.	• You jump to conclusions.
• You provide solutions that preserve dignity.	• You don't pause to consider factors that might be important to those involved.
• When someone confides in you, they know you will honor their privacy.	
Questions for Reflection:	
• Do people avoid telling you important information, or do they readily open up when they need someone to listen?	
• Do you listen with a preset conclusion in mind, or do you discipline yourself to listen and really hear what others are saying?	

Attentiveness

A large part of being trustworthy is being known as someone who shows attentiveness (see Reflection 3.8). This is shown through active listening and having the discipline to not interrupt others when they speak. This involves hearing the entirety of what someone has to say, even if—especially if!—they are struggling with finding words or with explaining things in a way that makes sense. It's easy to want to jump in and offer your interpretation and response, but if you really want a natural explanation from someone else, interrupting is something to be avoided. This is a weakness of mine. When someone is trying to tell me something, I will jump in to finish their sentences for them. Other times, I'll have an

Reflection 3.8 Attentiveness Reflection

Attentiveness	
A Strong Mindset: • You focus on the message others are trying to communicate. • You wait for others to finish. • You don't compete for voice time. • You don't think your words are more important than the words of others.	**Room for Growth:** • You feel you need to say something to be part of a conversation. • You feel anxiety if you can't respond point-for-point to someone else. • After a conversation, you can remember what you said but not what others said.
Questions for Reflection: • Are you easily distracted, or can you focus your energy and your mind on prioritized conversations and situations? • After listening to someone speak, do you often forget what words they used, or can you readily repeat what they've said?	

exciting thought I want to share immediately. But every time I interrupt, I regret it. There aren't many more disrespectful or unfair actions to take with another person than to stop their attempts to communicate or steal their voice. I constantly remind myself that what I have to say does not matter more than what someone else has to say. Not a child, not a parent, not a teacher. My input can wait until it's my turn. When I focus my attention on others, I can truly hear what they are thinking and feeling.

Clarity

When managing a conflict, listening without interruption is a bridge to clarity in vision when considering solutions (see Reflection 3.9). While

Reflection 3.9 Clarity Reflection

Clarity	
A Strong Mindset: • You know how to tier your involvement in managing conflict. • You think about your hoped-for outcomes before you act. • You consider your role and then are clear with yourself and others about what your involvement will be.	**Room for Growth:** • You cannot articulate a hoped-for outcome. • Others are unclear about the reasons for a particular action.
Questions for Reflection: • Do you go into conflict situations without a plan, or do you carefully consider your level of involvement and response? • Are others left in the dark about your planned response, or do you take time to articulate them?	

solutions will look different in every situation, principals might choose one of four actions to match an envisioned ideal outcome and the implementation of a plan to achieve that outcome. Figure 3.1 provides a few options, arranged by tier of intensity in involvement.

Do nothing. You learn about a conflict, evaluate the details, consider the impact on students and their learning, and decide no action is needed. The conflict will be handled by others or will dissipate on its own.

Orchestrate a conversation. You decide your role is to ask others to come together to discuss the problem and potential solutions. You know you don't need to be there; they can handle the conversation once they know you expect it to happen.

Oversee a conversation. In this case, you will organize discussion about a conflict, and you will join the conversation. Your role will be to sit, listen, and let others navigate the complications and resolution.

Facilitate a conversation. You identify yourself as the person to ensure everyone comes together, speaks in turn, and respectfully acknowledges others' perspectives. You start with introductions and a review of the conflict details, and then you will invite others to give their perspectives. You might ensure equal speaking-to-listening time, and, once a resolution seems possible, you will be the one to step in and wrap it up.

Figure 3.1 Tiers of Clarity

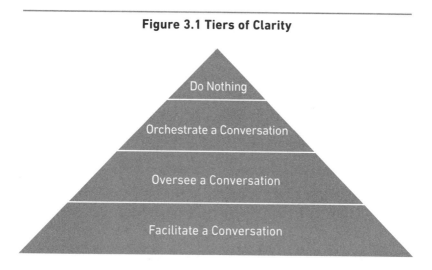

Equanimity

In spite of our best efforts for resolution, it's difficult to know exactly how much impact we've had on conflict. That's why equanimity is a valuable mindset to adopt (see Reflection 3.10). Composure during difficult times will allow us to accept when things are ambiguous or feel unsettled. After all, there are countless uncertainties in conflict management. Unlike many of the tasks of a principal—developing a master schedule, completing evaluations, developing and implementing professional development plans, overseeing facility updates—conflict management often has many loose ends and unmeasurable indicators of success. *How do you know if you're successful? Is success determined by the amount of people who complain? What they complain about? How angry they seem to be? How can you measure someone's feelings? What are the baselines, and how can someone's feelings be compared or contrasted to the feelings of other people?*

In addition to these unanswerable questions, there are times a conflict has been mediated and resolved, yet it resurfaces again later in a different form. Other times, it goes away and it's never spoken of again. It's impossible to predict the future, which is why sometimes a resolution means things are better *for now*—and that is good enough, especially if

Reflection 3.10 Equanimity Reflection

Equanimity	
A Strong Mindset:	**Room for Growth:**
• You accept outcomes without judgment on others. • You rest well knowing your input made a difference. • You understand there is not always a clean and clear wrap-up to problems between people.	• You revisit and reimagine outcomes, wishing things had turned out differently. • You second-guess the role you played and wonder what else can be done. • You get rattled when challenged by others or when you cannot thoroughly resolve a conflict.

Questions for Reflection:
• When conflict occurs, does it bother you, or are you able to accept it as a challenge to work through?
• Do you find yourself devoting time and energy to conflict even when you're not at work, or are you able to compartmentalize it?
• Do you try to overmanage conflict, or do you recognize there are things you cannot control about it?

you know you're up for mediating and addressing future residual problems that might pop up. As an additional bonus, a mindset of equanimity can bring peace to the work because we can remember that the outcome, however difficult or unexpected, however challenging and exhausting, will end up all right. If you believe this to be true—really believe it—you will have a more calm and confident approach to managing any conflict that crosses your path.

Character

In leadership, everything we do matters. What we say, how we say it, how we present ourselves to others, how we model problem solving and interpersonal relationships—all of those behaviors carry weight (see Reflection 3.11). I was once presenting at a conference and spoke about the importance of character. I told the attendees, "As we all know, character is explained as the choices we make when no one is watching." Then, without even realizing I was going to say it, I added, "But when you're a principal, someone is *always* watching." It's true. A principal's character is always under watch. Knowing this, it can feel like a tremendous amount of pressure to exhibit integrity in all situations; on the other hand, it is comforting to know you just need to do what you feel is right—every day, every time.

Reflection 3.11 Character Reflection

Character

A Strong Mindset:	Room for Growth:
• You are drawn to doing the right thing, even when it's not the easy thing. • When facing a conflict, others ask you for advice and guidance. • You aren't afraid of scrutiny or criticism.	• When making decisions, you are tempted or swayed by outside pressure (such as politics and power dynamics). • You fall into cycles of drama, gossip, or favoring particular teachers, students, and parents.

Questions for Reflection:
• Do you struggle to determine what path to take, or are you able to identify the "right thing" and then act on it?
• Are you insecure or confident in knowing what response is best?
• Do you waver when others scrutinize your decisions, or do you stay the course?

Acceptance

The final mindset we'll consider in this chapter is one of acceptance (see Reflection 3.12). In mastering this mindset, you will understand your influence potential. You will accept that there are things you cannot change, no matter what you do, how you do it, and what you say. You will be deliberate with your time to avoid spending it on things that don't matter. This is, of course, a version of a peace-filled equanimity mindset we discussed—if you protect your time and energy by not wasting it, and if you accept what control and influence you have, you will be a stronger leader.

Reflection 3.12 Acceptance Reflection

Acceptance	
A Strong Mindset: • You focus on the place between what matters and what influence you have. • Time you spend is productive for others.	**Room for Growth:** • You spend large amounts of time on problems but get very little results. • You try to control things that you cannot, or you try to control things that don't matter.
Questions for Reflection: • Do you spend a lot of time on things that don't have much impact, or are you able to focus on things that matter to your students, staff, and community? • Are you sometimes unable to identify priorities, or are you confident in how you prioritize your time?	

I came face-to-face with this lesson a few years ago. I was making changes to staff room assignments and needed to have two teachers share a room. This wasn't new; our building was over capacity, so many teachers were sharing space. I spoke with an intervention teacher and an English language teacher, explaining what room they would have together. I was taken aback by their reactions. Instantly resistant, both said the proposed changes simply would not work. It seemed they'd been in passive conflict for years, tracing back to some sharp words exchanged years earlier. I hadn't known about the friction between them, so I hadn't expected their resistance. No matter, I thought; I'd help them get through it. But regardless of what I did—individual conversations, shared meetings, strongly worded emails, intervention from myself and the guidance counselor—neither would budge. If anything, it increased their conflict, and their behavior started to resemble that of surly teenagers. I was so deflated that my efforts at getting them aligned had failed. I stressed. I fretted. I worried. I'd rarely failed at mediating a conflict, so I felt powerless. I didn't know how to proceed.

Just when I was out of ideas, I had a serendipitous moment. I thought about what mattered to our school—moving past conflict so we could better serve our students—and how that overlapped with the influence I had to manage the two teachers. The intersection of these two questions, I realized, was where I should focus my energy.

I asked myself the questions based on Figure 3.2. Did their conflict matter? Well, sort of. If they shared a room, their rift could cause culture problems in our school. Yet it seemed most staff thought the conflict was silly and pointless and thus weren't affected by it. To my knowledge, everyone just ignored it. Students were not affected; the conflict wasn't about them, didn't happen in front of them, and didn't affect their school experience. In other words, their conflict actually didn't matter all that much.

Figure 3.2 Finding Your Productive Focus

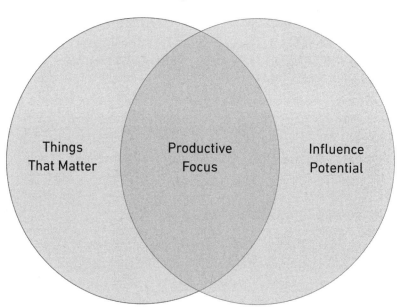

Things
That Matter

Productive
Focus

Influence
Potential

On the other side was the question of what potential influence I had. Did I have any influence over how they interacted? Again, sort of. I could expect them to behave as professionals, but I couldn't control how rigid they both were, and I couldn't control if they decided to keep fighting or if they decided to forgive one another.

What was left, then, was the part in the middle. What should I focus on that would be productive for the two teachers, their colleagues, and their students? The solution came quickly and clearly. I could shift the English language teacher to a different grade level, looping her up with her current caseload, and she would share a space with her new grade-level team. I would put two paraprofessionals in the classroom shared by the intervention specialist. No one got a room on their own, so there was no free pass; there were consequences for both because of their inability to resolve their conflict. Yet they would be in different parts of the building, working with different subsets of students, so their paths would rarely cross. Just like that, I got all my headspace back. I had productive focus that allowed me to make the right move, and in doing so, I accepted that the outcome was the best solution for everyone involved. The teachers mirrored my mindset, and both happily accepted this decision, and we didn't need to speak of it again.

These mindsets will all be factors in mediating conflict. Some are more effective than others, depending on the situation and the people involved, but all are helpful in keeping yourself calm and focused when working through conflicts.

As a next step, let's move into Chapter 4 to study a three-step process for managing conflict. This process, which involves *anticipating* conflict, *analyzing* its probable impact, and *acting* on a response, can be utilized any time a conflict emerges and will help ground the work of helping others get along. As you read, remind yourself what we've discussed in this chapter and consider how a principal's interpersonal skills can be embedded into each part of the process.

4

Anticipate, Analyze, Act: A Process for Mediating Conflicts

In Chapter 1 and Chapter 2, we discussed the origins and manifestations of conflict. We also considered what leadership character mindsets help in successfully managing it. In this chapter, let's outline three specific steps principals might follow when responding to conflict in their schools.

As a starting point, let's consider whether conflict management can actually fit into a neat, clean process. The answer is . . . sometimes. Every conflict is unique, with its own antecedents and implications, and each has unique variations of personalities, maturity levels, outlooks, and desired outcomes. With so many incalculable variables, the process needs to be circular and continuous (see Figure 4.1). Rather than think of it as a start-to-finish exercise, you can enter the circle at any point. Thinking through each part of the circle will ensure a thorough understanding of the conflict and provide a clear path forward. With enough practice, these steps can become part of a guide for conversation with staff, students, and families. This chapter is broken into three parts, each of which will dive deeper into the steps to managing conflict in your school.

Figure 4.1 The Anticipate-Analyze-Act Cycle

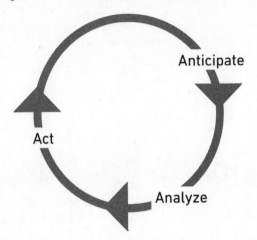

The first step is to *anticipate*. So many conflicts are predictable—not necessarily the specific people or details, but there are many situations that share similar components. Accepting the inevitability of conflicts allows us to see them coming, which can be a first—and recurring—step to managing them. Second, principals can *analyze* the reasons and repercussions of conflict and determine what interventions and input, if any, they should provide. After that, the principal can *act* to intervene, mediate, and help resolve the conflicts. This step includes applying what was learned, which sets up a neat entry back around the circle in preparing for future conflicts.

Let's start right at the beginning. How can principals anticipate typical conflicts?

Step One: Anticipate

Conflicts are guaranteed to occur, which means we need not be taken aback when they arise. In fact, we can anticipate scenarios in which conflicts are likely and work to reduce their frequency or complexity.

When I was a young administrator, I would angst about problems that came my way, both personally and professionally. Each time I had a problem solved, I would feel good about myself for about three minutes—and then another problem would unexpectedly pop up, and I would be both surprised and overwhelmed by the task of eliminating it. It was a continuous, exhausting game of whack-a-mole. It was my father—not an educator, but wise in this type of thing—who observed my tendencies and advised me to think differently. "Life and work are just one long series of problems to solve," he said. "Your approach is to try to *eliminate* all problems. It's much healthier to *embrace* problems as they come." He was right. Working through problems, one after another, is not so stressful if your mind accepts each as just one of an ongoing string of problems, with another one likely coming around the corner. This approach, in which we don't seek to eliminate problems but instead embrace the never-ending process of solving them, has been an important mind shift for me. In time, I've learned not only to accept a cycle of problem solving, but also to recognize that solving them comes more easily and efficiently if I predict and prepare for them. Knowing they are coming helps me achieve clarity and consistency in solving them.

As a principal, there are conflicts you can count on:

- Student fights, arguments, threats, and social discord
- Students in complicated social situations or relationships
- Students who are the victims of bullying or engage in bullying behavior
- Students who compete for placement in an academic, social, athletic, or extracurricular hierarchy
- Students whose parents get involved in their social challenges
- Parents who are frustrated with a teacher's approach, classroom management, discipline procedures, or communication
- Parents who hear news about their child that they do not want to hear
- Parents whose communication expectations are not aligned with the teacher's communication approach
- Parents whose professional or domestic situations are in friction with school needs
- Teachers who have a philosophy, approach, or style misaligned with other teachers

- Teachers frustrated by colleagues who do not adhere to the school's general norms and expectations
- Teachers who feel a sense of unfair or unequal workloads

These conflicts are common, universal, and—yes—predictable. Any principal scanning that list can likely recall scenarios related to each one of them, complete with names, faces, history, and outcomes. And any principal can probably scan that list and identify conflicts that might be brewing, right this minute.

Many of us naturally predict conflict and make moves to avoid a repeat. Let's consider a common example. Each summer, when principals begin developing teacher–student assignments for the coming year, they know there are certain students and parents who might not do well with a particular teacher's approach. As a result, they—or their designee, such as a guidance counselor or team of teachers—develop rosters with an eye for avoiding conflicts throughout the year. They do the same with students. They know which students should be separated, which students work well together, and how the individual social needs of each child can be proactively addressed by placement with the right peers. This thoughtfulness is an example of predicting conflict and making moves to avoid it.

The same anticipatory work can be done with teachers. Principals can take care to predict which collegial pairings might be successful and which ones might not. When I was first hired as a teacher, the principal offered me the job and, in the same sentence, said, "And I know exactly who I want you to work with." She knew I would be a great fit with a particular team leader, who indeed turned out to be a dear mentor and friend. When principals deliberately pair teachers with people with whom they will work well, they not only enhance camaraderie and teamwork, they also avoid collegial conflict. This isn't to say principals shouldn't count on teachers to successfully work with anyone; basic professionalism should ensure that a principal does not need to micromanage teacher teams or department placements.

Even knowing that conflict is a frequent and natural result of human relationships, it helps to predict potential personality or professional discord. A friend of mine told me one of the biggest mistakes she made as a principal was to put four "alpha" teachers on the same team. Each one was a bold, confident, aggressive, experienced teacher leader. "They all wanted to be in charge," she said, "but as I watched them, I was reminded of the phrase 'You're not a leader if no one is following.' Each had strong personalities and were confident they had the right ideas, skills, and experience to take charge in any situation. None were willing to sit back, compromise, and let things just happen. They were constantly in conflict." My friend wished she'd predicted the personality clash and placed the teachers on different teams, as it would have saved an enormous amount of time and emotional energy that had to be dedicated to their ongoing disagreements. The next year, the principal was able to rectify the situation by moving the teachers to different teams; still, she felt regret. In their new assignments, each of the teachers had to start over again with new team dynamics and new collegial relationships. "I feel like they each lost a year or two," she said. Improving the situation took time and patience—and probably could have been avoided altogether.

Anticipating conflict is not a perfect science, as there is no way to know when it will occur. It's still worth a little proactive consideration, because making moves to lessen or eliminate it will create a more peaceful and calm working environment and save a lot of work later. Now, how do you prepare for conflict?

Put Systems in Place

Developing standardized systems, processes, and protocols can all help principals prepare for conflict. In a practical example of proactive implementation, principals might work with a leadership team to develop a solid discipline referral system, outlining what exactly teachers should do when they encounter conflicts between students. Are teachers, guidance counselors, and support staff trained to intervene and support the students? When students get in a fight, how is the referral handled? In a similar example, developing a schoolwide system of regular communication—clear expectations for use of newsletters, emails, websites, and social media—will help engage parents and hopefully provide trusting, ongoing two-way connections when something goes wrong. Outlining specific steps and making them universally understood will trigger a fair, equitable response to conflict.

Look for Patterns

If the same situation keeps arising again and again, searching for the common denominator might help. When you study discipline data, for example, you might see a consistent uptick in student conflict right before extended holiday breaks. When you are tracking student transiency rates, you might notice that teachers get testy with one another when there is an influx of new student move-ins. In the former situation, students may experience increased stress before a long break; in the latter, frequent new students might create lopsided roster distribution. There are hundreds of possible scenarios, based on each school's systems, but it helps to identify trends in your school so you can predict an increase in conflicts—and prepare your response.

Empower Others

Principals cannot be the only person to whom others look for resolution and management of conflict. Most teachers are naturally skilled at listening and supporting students and colleagues, and they can all act as conflict managers when needed. Empowering staff to lead and model conflict management takes a heavy load off the principal's plate. For example, if a school's culture is one in which students get sent to the principal's office for even the smallest classroom infractions, the principal will never get out from under the constant referrals. That's why low-level student disagreements should be handled by the teacher or staff member most directly involved. Investigation, mediation, and follow-through can occur right there in the moment, and the issue never needs to rise to an office referral. The same applies to staff conflicts. Every staff member should feel willing and able to address conflict immediately and at the source of the problem. If colleagues are disagreeing in a way that affects others, it doesn't necessarily need to involve the principal. In my experience, if someone brings a conflict to me that belongs back at the source, I've had success explaining, "That conflict is something that doesn't seem to require the principal's intervention. Let me know if you feel differently, but in the meantime, I'll stay out of the way and let you handle it."

Create a Culture That Welcomes Productive Conflict

When hundreds of people work together every day, there will inevitably be some conflict; however, if everyone knows it is to be expected, it isn't such a shock when it comes. Teachers need to be reminded of this. Many feel dismayed or disappointed when their students engage in conflict-inducing behaviors, especially if students are actively *seeking* conflict with one another or with teachers. I recall a student who had been diagnosed with an oppositional defiant disorder, a manifestation of an emotional disability category requiring explicit teaching and support. Even with this diagnosis, every time the student grew combative or insubordinate, his teacher—who prided herself in having a conflict-free classroom environment—felt like she had failed. In response, on my end, I consistently reminded her of the predictability of the event and coached her to work through each incident without showing her personal disappointment. Part of creating a conflict-welcome culture is reminding others that it is to be expected—and encouraging them to accept it when it comes. This culture will hopefully lead to calm, drama-free resolutions.

Step Two: Analyze

If the conflict is one that existing systems, people, or cultures cannot manage, the principal might need to analyze it more closely by learning about its antecedents and effects. Reliance on patience is wise here, as it is impossible to truly understand a nuanced conflict in just a few rushed minutes. Taking time to truly understand a conflict will frame the evaluation of response options.

Check Your State of Mind

Because a principal's job is often overrun with countless tasks, responsibilities, and concerns, it can be difficult to fully commit to managing conflict. When a conflict arises that seems to require my intervention, my first internal response is often frustration: "I don't have time for this." A weak state of mind—irritation, exhaustion, anger—can cloud my thinking and response, so I try to take a moment to ensure I am thinking clearly, am ready to focus, and can accurately analyze the situation. When I find myself resenting the necessity of my involvement, I give myself a little lecture: *Managing conflict is part of your job. You need to make time for it.* I remind myself that I actually enjoy working through tricky situations with others and offer a self-challenge to step up and lead toward a positive outcome.

Review the Feelings

When we investigate a conflict, we will uncover many accompanying emotions—after all, how people act is a by-product of how they feel. Understanding the depth and range of feelings will help explain why the conflict is personal and impactful for everyone involved. I recall a conflict in which one student caught another student using his earbuds, so he lashed out physically. I summarized my understanding of his feelings: "I know you feel the other student stole your earbuds, and that made you very upset. Would you like to tell me more about that?" The student talked for a long time about feeling wronged, violated, and disrespected. It helped us both to understand the role anger had played in the events leading up to the altercation.

Review the Facts

While acknowledging the depth and range of feelings is important, compiling facts is even more so. In some ways, analyzing conflict requires a clinical approach, with verified facts as primary tools. We will want to learn who is involved, where the problem started, what has been said, what actions have been taken thus far, and the impact of the current situation. It takes skill to separate feelings from fact. In a conflict between students, I might say, "Thank you for explaining how angry you were about the student stealing your earbuds. Now let's review your reaction. What happened first? What happened after that?" By separating the facts and feelings, you'll have two pieces of important information. You will know the role feelings played in the conflict, but you'll also have clarity in facts—which will help you determine the level of intervention needed.

Gather Perspectives

Facts aren't always easy to verify. If you are stuck in the middle of a "he said, she said" conflict, and both sides are in a stalemate about what happened, you will need to reach out to others involved to identify what they know or what they saw. You'll want to be aware of bias and get input that is comprehensive and well-balanced. Years ago, I worked through an investigation of a lunchroom fight between two students. When I asked their teacher for information about possible antecedents, I knew she'd already been frustrated with one of the students. He'd been increasingly disruptive in class for weeks, making her quick to assume the fight was all his fault. When reviewing facts leading up to this specific incident, though, the teacher admitted she might be misplacing blame because of her bias, prompting us to seek perspective from the students' other teachers, the guidance counselor, and a coach who had both students on his team. We learned the fight was definitely two-sided, as the supposed target of the fight had been needling the aggressor for many months. In the end, we determined both students were equally responsible. Speaking to multiple people involved in a conflict will help enrich your overall understanding of it.

Discard Irrelevant Perspectives

You'll want to avoid getting bogged down by input from people who aren't directly involved or affected. In learning about a complicated conflict between staff members, a principal friend of mine once found herself approached by a third staff member who'd appointed herself the spokesperson of her colleague. My principal friend wisely said, "I need to hear directly from the person involved." The spokesperson still sat in the room during the investigation, supporting her friend, but the principal took care to speak directly to the person with a problem—making for a fairer and more thorough gathering of information.

Another example, frequently experienced by principals, is a phenomenon I have ruefully named "crowdsourcing complaints." We have all experienced this hundreds of times: The complainant shares their issue and then points out how many other people feel the same way. Every single time I've had to intervene in a conflict between a parent and an athletic coach, I've heard some version of these words: "I'm not the only parent who feels this way. Everyone else does too, but they're too worried to come forward." This might be true, but it is also quite possible that this parent spoke with some other parents, perhaps in the bleachers after one of the games, and the other parents nodded agreement—out of friendship, camaraderie, or because it was the easiest response to offer. With this "agreement," the original complainant feels validated and less alone; they also feel bolstered in their position and thus eager to quote "everyone else." My answer in these cases is always the same: "In this conversation, we'll focus on the concerns you have with your child's experience. If other parents have an issue, I hope they will come to me so we can discuss concerns they have about their child."

Listen, Listen, Listen

It's easy to *try* to listen. It's a lot more difficult to actually do it. When I feel rushed, or when I assume I already know all the facts of a situation, I struggle to truly, deeply, and thoroughly hear the perspectives of others. Yet, by forcing myself to slow down, listen, ask questions, and restate what I have learned, I can be confident that I thoroughly understand what happened and who had what role in the development of the problem.

Determine the Breadth of the Problem

Often, something that seems like a big deal, well ... *isn't*. I have a principal friend who often remarks, "Sometimes people bring me flames, but I only see sparks." Sparks can, of course, turn into flames—or they might fade to nothing. Taking time to determine how deep the problem really is can often bring clarity in response. You might analyze answers to these questions:

- Is everyone safe?
- Is someone hurt? Is the hurt physical, emotional, or both?
- Is there lasting damage?
- Does someone feel threatened?
- Is this about perceived territory or competition, or has someone truly stepped out of line?

- Are the allegations true?
- Can the allegations be verified?
- Are there witnesses?

Brainstorm Solutions Together

It's easy to think that resolving a conflict should involve a sit-down mediation to talk it out. Not necessarily. There are many other ways to solve a conflict, and gathering alternate ideas can be very helpful. I will often ask, "Now that we know the problem, what solutions do you see?" This gives power to those who are involved. A few years ago, my sister, a teacher in a virtual school, had a disagreement with one of her colleagues. The two had exchanged heated emails, both expressing their exasperation with one another. Upset and hurt, my sister called me to process the situation. "I just don't see a way forward," she said. I listened as she vented then suggested we brainstorm some options. We found some: the two could agree to a pause in emails for a few days until emotions had cooled; they could set up a virtual meeting to discuss face-to-face; they could create a document of potential compromises to share with one another. In the end, the two actually did all three of these actions and worked through their issues peacefully. Brainstorming solutions is always better when it's not done in isolation, because new ideas and suggestions are the key to solving problems in unique ways. I am constantly reminded of this—just when I think I have exhausted every possible idea, if I ask for input from others, I invariably get something new, creative, or innovative I would never have thought of on my own.

Plan a Response

Once you have a firm grasp on the antecedents to the current situation, you'll want to plan your next steps. The important part here is to consider desired outcomes. First, of course, you want everyone to get along. You also want to come out of the conflict with everyone better off—to have learned something, improved something, or to be better able to work well together. Your plan should include what you, as the leader, will do; what you will ask others to do; how you will apply solutions and follow through; and specific steps and timeline for communicating the responsibilities and expectations for others.

Intervene Early

When a conflict is brewing, it is often difficult to know when it might turn into something bigger. This is a good time to enforce the Four Tens idea outlined in Chapter 2. If something will not matter in 10 minutes or 10 hours, you might want to let it go. If it will cause damage 10 months or 10 years from now, you'll want to step in.

Step Three: Act

The third step to conflict management is to *act*. You may need to adjust the plan as you go along to allow for unexpected changes, moods, and emerging strong feelings, but a single action step will start the ball rolling. But there are a few things to keep in mind.

No Action Is an Action

Sometimes, upon analyzing the situation, principals might recognize that there is no direct intervention needed. This is a perfectly acceptable course of action. I think of the time I received an email from an upset parent who expressed frustration with a particular teacher's homework policy. I replied that I was sorry she was frustrated, and I encouraged her to reach out directly to the teacher, who would be the best person to respond. I let the teacher know the parent would be in touch. But the teacher never heard from the parent—not that day, and not in the days or weeks that followed. I had a decision to make—should I continue to push the parent to contact the teacher? Should I respond to the allegations in her email, even though there was no specific evidence of a problem? I went back and reread the email and found no direct question, request, or verifiable concerns, so I let it go. I did nothing. For the rest of the year, neither the teacher nor myself heard from that parent. We realized the email must have been sent in a moment of anger between parent and child, and the recipient of the anger—the teacher—did not actually have a role in its creation or solution. If the problem will go away on its own—minor, inconsequential disagreements come to mind here, as do accusations with no evidence—it is perfectly acceptable for the principal to rely on existing systems to let the problem work itself out.

Big Problem = Big Action

Of course, as mentioned earlier, there are some incidents in which taking no action would be a mistake. Some conflicts require swift and decisive intervention. Principals should consider what are the non-negotiables for their schools—what interpersonal incidents simply will not be tolerated—and draw a mental line between which conflicts will heal with time, support, and space, and which ones must be immediately managed. Physical attacks, ongoing intent to harm, anything involving threats or weapons—these will all require a strong, decisive, and impactful action from the principal.

Set the Environment

If you do decide you need to intervene, you'll start by deciding where to gather those with whom you plan to discuss the solution. Many times, we fall back on meeting in the principal's office. If that setting causes anxiety or high emotions for anyone involved, you might consider a different venue. Years ago, I worked with a mother who was in a bitter custody battle and her child was exhibiting angry outbursts at school. I'd met with her a couple times about her child's behavior, and each time, I found her to be tense and anxious. On one unseasonably warm spring day, she'd been called to come pick up her child, and I happened to be at the front door when she arrived. Spontaneously, I invited her to talk on an outside bench that was hidden behind the athletic wing. We had a very productive conversation. At the end, as we reviewed our agreed-upon path forward, I couldn't help but remark on the improved tone of our conversation. She said, "Being in the principal's office makes me feel like I'm in my attorney's office, and I can't get out of that mindset. I much prefer meetings somewhere else." When parents or students are anxious about sitting across from the principal's desk, it's easy to adjust the seating in the room, choose another room, or find another setting altogether. Again, you'll want to think through your hoped-for outcome and decide what setting will help you meet your goals.

Set Your Intentions

When responding to conflict, I find it helpful to specifically articulate an ideal outcome. I might open the conversation by saying, "After this meeting, I'd like to know we have acknowledged the problem and have a mutually acceptable path forward." I ask others to share their hopes as well and make a point of referencing them throughout the conversation. A simple phrase like "Let's start with what we are hoping to accomplish today" can keep the focus on a productive outcome.

Acknowledge All Sides

Disagreements, discord, and misunderstandings are often rooted in someone feeling they aren't seen or heard. When listening to someone in conflict, I will often say, "Can I say this back to you? I want to make sure I have it right." In group conversations, I'll say, "I'd like to try to capture what I'm hearing by paraphrasing it for everyone to hear. If I don't have something right, please speak up, because I want to be sure every perspective is acknowledged." Even if I think a particular side is misguided, I'll still speak to it, thus acknowledging its presence and its validity.

A few years ago, I had to investigate a fight between two students. One student was clearly the aggressor, and video showed her attack the other student unprompted and without warning. While talking with her and gathering the perspectives of others, I knew it was important to acknowledge her side. "You felt the other girl was talking about you behind your back, turned your best friend against you, and was plotting to 'take' your other friends too. It made you extremely upset, and you felt you had to do something to stop it." Although the student ended up with a suspension for her physical aggression, it helped her—and her parents—to know that I truly did understand how she'd been feeling in the moment she attacked the other girl.

Clear Communication

In finalizing a resolution, you'll want to ensure everyone has the right information by saying it out loud, checking for understanding and verifying agreement. One strategy is to say, "Let's quickly go around and have each person explain what their next steps will be." If the conflict involves adults, it can help to follow up with a group email outlining what our resolution is and how each person will contribute to the solution.

Rehearse

Not long ago, a principal friend asked me to meet her for a cup of coffee. She needed to intervene with a staff conflict, and she was nervous. The situation had been simmering for a while. One teacher had hung a "Merry Christmas" placard on the wall in an area she shared with a colleague. That colleague did not celebrate Christmas and did not believe any reference to religious holidays should be evident in school. The first teacher refused to take down the sign, and the second teacher got upset every time she saw it. Over coffee, I pretended to be each staff member, and my friend rehearsed what she would say to them. I alternated using the point of view of each respective teacher, asking difficult questions and even role-playing some responses my friend might encounter—eye rolling, interrupting, and a raised voice. My friend was much more prepared for the conversation because she'd practiced potential versions ahead of time.

Adjust as Needed

Even the best plans will need to be adjusted and amended as you implement them. Any number of things can happen along the way to change your course of action. You'll gain further information; you'll verify facts or be able to discard irrelevant information; you'll run into barriers you hadn't expected; or you might see the problem is more complicated—or, if you're lucky, less complicated—than you'd thought.

Years ago, when I was an English teacher, a parent was frustrated because her child's homework assignments were often missing. Eager to help, I promised the parent I would initial the student's planner every single day. I found myself missing days, though, because the chaos and challenges of the day would interfere with my promise. The parent was understandably frustrated with me, feeling I wasn't prioritizing her child's challenges. We made the slightest little tweak: The student would be asked to initial the planner himself, bring it to me at the end of the period, and I would add a checkmark. Moving the responsibility to the student was a strategy the parent couldn't argue with, and it made me successful in the role I'd promised. Sometimes solutions need a small tweak; other times, the whole plan might need to be reevaluated. Being someone willing to adjust the plan, especially if it isn't working as hoped, is a sign of leadership wisdom.

Follow Through

After a plan is established and implemented, applying it requires follow-through. This can be done formally, informally, or both. As an added bonus, following through provides an opportunity to make any long-term changes to systems and processes as a result of what you've learned from the conflict. Here are a few ways principals can wrap up the action in a conflict mediation process:

Document

As mentioned earlier, and particularly in conflicts involving adults, I sometimes take notes along the way and then summarize them into a shared document or an email. I send it to all adults involved in the resolution. I write the message in a friendly and positive tone, outlining everything that was agreed upon and summarizing any responsibilities or promises that were agreed upon during the meeting.

Formal Check-ins

Formal check-ins ensure the outcome proceeds as planned. It might involve a prescheduled in-person meeting or could simply be a shared document in which updates are noted, dated, and monitored. In the case of student conflict, it might mean benchmarks met and tracked on a clipboard, or it might include follow-up meetings with the teacher or school counselor. A trick I use is to create an event on my calendar to be repeated at regular intervals, reminding me to follow up. When I feel the issue is resolved, I delete the event.

Informal Check-ins

Potentially more powerful than formal conversations, casual and unplanned check-ins are especially informative because they are random—prohibiting an inauthentic response. You might take advantage of seeing someone in the hall, at lunch, or after school to ask, "How are things going now that we have implemented our plan?"

Shift Ownership to the Owner

As mentioned earlier, the principal isn't the only person who should absorb ordinary conflict and its resolution. Once a conflict has been thoughtfully considered and received the attention it warrants, those involved can be empowered to seek positive outcomes for themselves; after all, when it comes to the more unexceptional disagreements and frustrations that are the standard fare of living and working alongside others, the only reactions we can control are our own.

Not long ago, after working through a complicated complaint from one staff member about another, I checked in with her and found she was still struggling with her perception of how the other person was handling it. I told her, kindly and carefully, "You are the only person in charge of your personal and professional happiness. You can't expect to have a conflict-free life, but by owning your role in solutions, you can expect a peaceful one." Her professional contentment was in her hands. "Don't let someone else steal your peace," I said. "It's yours to lose . . . or keep." Reminding others of the power they have to write their own ending takes responsibility off of you and puts it where it belongs—on those who are struggling with the conflict in the first place.

Commitment vs. Compliance

Often, those involved in a conflict can easily comply with mandated expectations. It's much more difficult to truly commit to a resolution. Anyone who has tried to resolve a student conflict by asking those involved to "stay away from each other" knows this. Students may try to comply for a day or two, but then they seem to just find each other, like magnets that can't go any other way. This happens when we use "stay away" as an intervention between a bully and a victim. It just doesn't work; not only is it insufficient justice for the victim, but the bully gets more stealthy, and the victim gets more anxious, upset, and isolated. Instead, those involved should be reminded of the difference between *complying* with the solution and *committing* to it. Ideally, both actions are necessary—solutions should be *compliance rooted in commitment.* If the solution isn't working, I circle back to analyze which one needs some work.

Teach

Someone once told me, "People only battle in one direction." It's true; when in conflict, people get further and further entrenched into their side of the situation. To learn from conflict, principals may need to directly teach others how to battle in both directions—to see both sides, validate one another, and accept different perspectives. We want to encourage others to be part of two-sided solutions, mediations, and conclusions. It is everyone's job to deal with conflict and everyone's job to avoid reliving tug-of-war games, which can be done by learning and applying what we've learned.

Improve

Conflict has immense value when it leads to updating and improvement of processes. If there are recurring problems that can be attributed to outdated or weak protocols, conflict can be the impetus to improvement. Without conflict, it's hard to see areas that need improvement; after all, when inefficient processes are normalized and no one questions why, it is difficult to see any other way. Conflict can remove these blinders and lead to growth and change.

Before we move on from this chapter, let's circle back to the mindsets we discussed in Chapter 3. When joining the circle of *anticipate-analyze-act,* you'll want to do a quick audit of how your mindset is guiding you. I use a notebook to jot down quick notes, and it's always within reach. I've taped a list of these mindsets to the notebook, and it serves as a visual reminder for me. Just a quick skim of the list in Figure 4.2 will help you calm your mind and recalibrate to a place of productive focus.

As stated earlier, being a principal means having a constant, ongoing dose of problems to solve, and the circle of steps outlined here are a way to systematically approach conflict. Conflict will always be part of the work of education, and because eliminating it is not an option, the sequence to anticipate, analyze, and act will provide the structure and systems needed to manage it. In the next chapter, we begin to study specific, common conflicts principals will need to mediate, starting with those that occur between teachers.

Figure 4.2 Mindsets

MINDSETS		
Patience	Confidence	Clarity
Poise	Empathy	Equanimity
Eloquence	Trust	Character
Curiosity	Attentiveness	Acceptance

5

Conflicts Between
Teachers

Many principals aspire to have their schools be a conflict-free workplace, often measuring themselves against those expectations. *If the adults in the building can't get along,* they wonder, *what does that say about me as a leader? Wouldn't a strong principal have a school built on camaraderie and peaceful collaboration?*

Well, sort of. Principals can work to establish a culture of professional collegiality and provide a clear *anticipate-analyze-act* process to address conflicts, but they will still need to manage personality differences, background baggage, and emotional entanglements that complicate professional relationships—which are, of course, subject to the same challenges present in any human relationship.

Ideally, professional relationships develop and grow in simple, natural, and reciprocal ways. They endure various challenges and get stronger with time. They might even grow into deep and lifelong friendships. On the other hand, some professional relationships are fraught with friction. Colleagues argue, disagree, hold grudges, and take one another for granted. Sometimes these conflicts turn into problems that rise and fall with time; other times, especially when one staff member moves to a different location or job, the collegial relationship is no longer needed so it fizzles out and is forgotten, taking with it any lingering conflicts.

I once met a teacher friend for coffee after he found himself dealing with the emotional aftermath of an angry confrontation with a colleague. They hadn't spoken in weeks, and he was hoping to heal the rift between them. He wanted advice because he was deeply upset about how things had unfolded and knew his emotions were leading his response. He recognized he carried some responsibility for their argument, but he felt the other person owned some of it, too, and didn't know how to get started on a path to healing. He told me he felt like he was experiencing a breakup, with all the heartache, blame, and defensiveness that comes along with the end of a relationship. His district had a procedure for transfer requests, and so he knew he could request a different job placement, but he didn't want to leave his current school. He said, only half-joking, "I don't want a divorce, but I don't want to stay married, either. A separation is probably healthy, but we're going to have to get along for the kids." Much like many long-term relationships, collegial relationships do take effort and energy, and I applauded this teacher for recognizing he'd have to do some work to repair the damage.

In that case, the resolution came with the two colleagues discussing the argument, taking mutual responsibility, and agreeing to move on. It's a little more complicated when mending a rift requires a principal's intervention. The way I see it, there are two basic approaches. The first is to create an environment and culture in which teachers are empowered—expected, even—to work through issues on their own in a mature, calm, professional way. The second, which is necessary when the conflict grows too big to be managed internally, is to mediate directly. If principals dedicate themselves to the former, there will be very few instances of the latter because most problems will be taken care of before intervention even becomes a consideration.

This chapter will cover three considerations. First, we will discuss missteps principals make when they hear about conflict on their staff. Second, we will consider how to create a culture of natural internal mediation. Finally, we will implement the anticipate-analyze-act process, covered in Chapter 4, to work through potential direct intervention with teachers.

Common Missteps

As mentioned earlier, conflicts between teachers can interfere with a student's learning experience and can damage overall school culture. That's why principals hope for a conflict-free workplace and why they might panic a little when they catch wind of discord between teachers. Let's think of some missteps principals might make and why it's best to avoid them.

Intervening Unnecessarily or Too Soon

Just because someone thinks they need the principal's intervention does not mean they *actually* need that intervention. My third year of teaching, I got in a minor dust-up with a colleague. We were disagreeing about the logistics of an upcoming interdisciplinary unit. We exchanged sharp words that ended with one of us walking off in a huff. I was upset, as was the other teacher. We each separately vented to friends, but with time and space, we worked it out and were able to make some mutually beneficial adjustments to our plans. Neither of us ever heard from the principal, which was of great relief to me. Both my colleague and I considered the whole thing to be over. Later that year, the principal and I found ourselves standing side-by-side watching a student performance, and she asked how things were going with the other teacher after our "scuffle," as she called it. Fine, I said, but I admitted I was surprised she even knew about it. "I heard a few rumblings," she said, "but I felt no need to step in." It wasn't her business, she said; she knew we were adults and she treated us as such. Just as we don't always have to intervene with student disagreements, we should avoid intervening with adult ones too, unless there is a tangible, ongoing effect on school culture or student learning.

If the principal decides it is necessary to step in, it should only happen after other efforts have failed. Just as my principal trusted I could work out my disagreement with a colleague, we want to give teachers the time and space to manage their conflict. It's difficult to know for certain when a disagreement will turn into something bigger and less manageable, but jumping at the first sign of a problem will just create a culture in which it seems you are micromanaging the teachers. If anything, your intervention should be a last resort. Let teachers try to work it out. If they can't, you'll know.

Avoidance

It is true teachers should work to smooth over conflict whenever possible; indeed, there are several times in this book where I encourage principals to pause and let adults work out their problems. Yet it is important to note there are times the principal will need to intervene. If a staff member is being harassed, treated with hostility, or subject to bullying tactics from another member of the staff, it is the principal's responsibility to ensure the inappropriate or unprofessional behavior stops immediately. Too many times, perhaps because they don't know how to intervene or because the aggressor is cunning, confident, or powerful, principals will avoid the problem in the hope that things will calm down and work out. When I provide professional development to principals, I often remind them, "Hope is not a strategy." We can't simply avoid addressing problems by hoping it will get better. When someone is consistently being treated poorly by a colleague, avoidance is likely to make things worse and increase problems over time.

The Hero Syndrome

I used to think I should intervene in every staff conflict, because I genuinely thought I could fix anything with the right mindset, approach, and tone. This is a common misstep; many of us think we can convince everyone to think like we do, thus coming to the peaceful outcome we envision. In one of the most difficult conflicts I've ever mediated, a teacher was so angry at a colleague she seemed to have crossed into a place of emotional instability. I wasn't worried because I was certain I could fix it. I *wanted* to fix it. I wanted everyone to *know* I'd fixed it. So I went to talk to her. In my efforts to be a hero, I ended up making it worse. I intervened with an emotional person at an emotional time about an emotional event, and the things I said, in an effort to provide perspective, ruined any hope of repairing the relationship. Just as explained above, rather than try to be a hero, I should have paused on any action until I was certain emotions had calmed and cooled.

A Tattletale Culture

A friend of mine once remarked about the job of the principal, "It seems like someone is always feeling angry at someone else, and they are eager to bring the problem to the principal to solve." Part of the reason to hesitate on intervention is to avoid creating a culture in which disgruntled staff members rush to get the principal's attention. The thinking seems to be this: *If I get the principal on my side, it will be obvious that I am correct.* But if principals entertain "he said, she said" rundowns of internal conflict, they'll have to continue to do so. The unspoken message will be that the principal doesn't feel their staff is equipped to manage their own problems, so teachers will rush to get to the principal quickly—essentially telling on one another. I always find it ironic when teachers tattle on one another, because teachers tend to discourage tattling in their students unless it's necessary, and when it is, teachers are masterful in managing it. In fact, let's think a little more about young people as a way to better understand adults.

When children tell on one another, we think of it as a request for help. Imagine a typical lunchroom disturbance. A student approaches a teacher, reporting problematic behavior by a peer in hopes that the teacher will take their side and reprimand or punish the other student. But unless someone is in danger, teachers know not to swoop in and make themselves the solution. Instead, they help the student consider perspectives, options, and solutions. In empowering a child to work through a conflict, teachers give them the tools and confidence to proceed on their own. Tattling is a natural part of being a child, because children rely on adults to learn how to work through peer discord.

The same thinking must be applied when teachers tattle to the principal. When we are overly involved in resolving inconsequential disputes, we are effectively telling teachers we don't have faith in them to work it out. We essentially name ourselves as an official judge or jury—deciding who is right, deciding who is wrong, and offering a verdict to clarify the path forward. It sends the following unintended message:

- I do not believe the teachers can manage this conflict on their own.
- I do not trust them to come to a satisfactory outcome.
- I believe my input is necessary for a successful mediation or resolution.
- I will see the situation clearly, and I will respond appropriately.
- My decision will be the right and final one.

This is problematic in multiple ways. First, it assumes the principal has a full and fair understanding of the entire situation—what led to the conflict, what continues to feed it, and what the ideal outcome would be. Second, it takes away from the work a principal should be doing—supporting the student experience—and shifts their attention to an adult problem. Third, because of the uniquely positioned power dynamic of a supervisor intervening between subordinates, a principal's help might be perceived as overinvolvement or showing favor to certain staff members, which will divide them further.

For that reason, whenever possible, and assuming no one is unsafe, principals should discourage teachers from telling on one another. This is part of the *analyze* step in the process we discussed earlier. The principal might provide insight, perspective, and ideas for solutions—with the ultimate goal of encouraging staff members to work directly with one another to have open and productive dialogue.

Taking a Side

I once worked with a principal who had countless admirable traits. Her success was clouded by one big weakness. Before becoming the school's principal, she'd been a teacher in the building and had a close relationship with her teaching team. When she was awarded the role as principal, it was in large part due to the input of her previous teammates, who had launched an all-out campaign in support of her candidacy for the role. Given their outspoken support, it was likely a mistake to offer her the job; had the hiring committee anticipated future conflict, they may have provided her the opportunity to serve as a principal in a different building for a better fit. But there she was, and perhaps in return for the support of her previous coworkers during the hiring process, the new principal remained intensely loyal to them. They became her trusted confidants. She socialized with them, took advice from them, and vented to them. When disagreements arose, the principal would always side with those teachers. She was blinded by her loyalty, never even entertaining the idea that any of her former teammates could make a professional mistake. The rest of the staff knew this small group—nicknamed, in whispers, "The Untouchables"—would never be asked to shift or widen their thinking to accommodate perspectives of other staff members. The principal's propensity to side with certain teachers was damaging to the overall school culture.

With some of these common missteps under consideration, it's easy to see a throughline and learn from it. Principals should take care in how, when, and to what extent they will intervene in staff conflict. We'll discuss later how to best intervene when it *must* happen—as it sometimes does—but before that, let's consider a better option: empowering teachers to act as their own conflict managers. Let's discuss how principals create and lead a culture in which teachers resolve conflict in a professional, harmonious way.

Creating a Culture of Natural Internal Mediation

In my previous school, I was incredibly proud of the culture we'd built. Conflicts between teachers were rare, and when they happened, the teachers worked through them. There were teachers who weren't overly fond of one another, but they all coexisted peacefully and respectfully.

When I left, I was replaced by a principal who was—and still is—very different from me. Our leadership styles are poles apart. Yet, our hoped-for outcomes are exactly the same. He flourishes using his style of leadership, and the school still has the same vibe it did before; the teachers are positive, they work well together, and they address problems as they arise before they can turn toxic or damaging. The point here is that there is no magic formula for developing a positive collegial culture; instead, when principals bring their authentic selves, model how to manage complicated interactions, and establish high expectations for professionalism, their building staff will likely follow suit. Let's dig a little deeper into each of these concepts.

Be Authentic

There is not a clear checklist of what to do and what not to do in the principalship. The only must-do, in my view, is to be authentic and real. Being real makes it easier for teachers to connect to their leader, especially when conflict arises. An authentic principal is honest, open, transparent, vulnerable, and willing to be wrong. I know one principal who used to hide all her feelings, thinking a principal had to be stoic and unmoved in all settings. "I didn't have authentic connections with my teachers," she said, "until I finally let myself be who I am." These days, she will readily admit when she is frustrated, uncertain, or emotional. It helps teachers feel safe being their true selves, especially when in disagreement with their colleagues.

Model

Teachers are always watching how a principal handles conflict, and they mimic what they see. Indeed, they have plenty to see. Principals are immersed in conflict all the time, and most of it is not their doing. There have been many times I thought, "I had nothing to do with this problem, and I'm having to solve it!" I was once called to my supervisor's office because one of my staff members had given a state assessment outside an acceptable testing window. Although I hadn't even known the assessment was being administered, I was reprimanded. I was so upset I was shaking. I was mad at my boss for blaming me, mad at the staff member for the mistake, and mad that I conflicted with both of them—and, again, I hadn't personally done anything wrong. Stepping into the anticipate-analyze-act circle by carefully analyzing the situation, I knew what I needed to do: apologize for the mistake, mentor my staff member through it, and ensure the mistake was never repeated. As much as I wanted to yell, cry, and lash out in frustration, I took the evening to get my mind right so I could respond as I knew I should. My action was to meet with the staff member, explain why the mistake had caused an invalidation of the student's results, and brainstorm a checks-and-balances structure to avoid repeating it. I worked hard not to disparage my supervisor and did not let the issue grow into anything bigger than it needed to be. To be clear, it was not easy to handle the situation this way. I felt blamed for something I hadn't done, and I hated being in trouble with my boss. For several days, I was out of sorts, upset, and unable to stop thinking about it. I lost sleep. Outwardly, though, I modeled how I'd want someone else to behave. In time, the whole incident became just a memory, and I was so glad I hadn't reacted impulsively and damaged my relationship with my boss.

Change from "Yes, But" to "Yes, And"

In Chapter 2, we discussed the communication barrier that is created when we use a "yes, but" approach. Nothing before the *but* will be heard because *but* serves as a qualifier to anything that follows. Teaching others to use this approach can be done in a direct training, such as a "two-minutes of PD" model before a staff meeting, or by consistently pointing to your use of *and* instead of *but* in conversation. Before a tricky conversation, I will sometimes explain, "You'll hear me trying to use *and* instead of *but* when I look for solutions." When I succeed, I'll smile and say, "See how I did that?" Figure 5.1 offers a few examples of how this can be done.

Consider the Time of Year

It's no secret that teacher stress levels rise and fall with the challenges they face throughout the year. Not only are there times that a staff's collective stress increases—before holidays, when grades are due, when weather keeps people cooped up inside, when student behaviors escalate—but there are also school-specific situations that might create an increase in emotional impact. I once worked in a school where at both the beginning and middle of each year, we would analyze student data and make decisions about which students received Tier 2 intervention support. The system was unquestionably student-driven, and data helped us

Figure 5.1 "Yes, And"

Instead of	Say
I hear what you're saying, but I don't think that idea will work.	I hear what you're saying, and I actually agree with the points you're making. Another consideration is. . . .
This approach has worked in the past, but I don't see how it applies here.	This approach has worked in the past, and I wonder, how we can capitalize on its success in this situation?
You say you want this to be a collaboration, but I don't see that in your actions.	You say you want this to be a collaboration, and I'd love to think about how we can be equals in this work.
That makes sense in theory, but I don't see it working.	That makes sense in theory, and I think there might be creative ideas to make it come to action.
It's a good idea, but we've tried it before, and it was a failure.	It's a good idea, and we've tried it before. I wonder, why did it fail?
You are enthusiastic but not realistic.	Your enthusiasm is infectious. Who might we recruit to make sure we can bring this idea to reality?

ensure students who truly qualified for the intervention received it. Students who did not qualify for services were to receive appropriate differentiated Tier 1 support in the classroom. The only negative aspect of our process was the inevitable frustration felt by some teachers when they had students for whom they strongly felt needed Tier 2 support. They based this on their own anecdotal or qualitative classroom data, but that information was not considered in the quantitative approach we used. It was stressful for teachers, so sometimes they would fuss and snap at one another in advocacy of their students. I could predict it as clearly as the tides. Usually, I just let it ride out, and in a day or two things calmed down. In time, though, I learned to proactively address the upcoming conflict: "This is the time of year we get a little fussy at each other. Let's remember that all decisions are made from data. The decision-making team follows the same qualifying standards for all students. Please don't take it personally if it feels like your student gets the short shrift. Instead of going at each other, please bring any questions to any member of the team so we can give you the information behind these decisions." Predicting and planning for a brief rise in conflicts helped me openly discuss them, which strengthened our culture of collegiality.

Avoid Gossip-Based Reports

When teachers aren't getting along, a principal might hear about it from those who are not directly involved. But if the principal responds using unverified information, it becomes a game of telephone. An event happens, and it is told and retold until the facts of the situation are lost. Principals often have a few trusted staff members who give them a heads-up when something disturbing is brewing, but if these warnings are based in gossip or chatter, it will be difficult to formulate an appropriate response. That's why I avoid responding to hearsay, trying instead to only use firsthand accounts of an incident.

Remember the Bigger Picture

Educators focus on students. Although working with others is part of that, I believe we spend an enormous amount of time in education on things that don't have a direct and positive impact on students. Remembering the students helps reorient our focus. If teachers' planning periods are spent talking about one another and stirring up conflict, they are not spending that time planning for, or working with, the students who need them. Principals can keep the spotlight on students by modeling and highlighting a mindset of student-centered decisions, conversation, and problem solving.

Principal Intervention

Even with a strong overall culture of professionalism, there are times the principal does need to intervene directly between staff who are in conflict and unable to come to a resolution. If the conflict is affecting the student experience, or if there is widespread damage to the overall school culture, waiting for the problem to work out on its own might be a mistake. In these situations, the principal will enter the anticipate-analyze-act process with specific active intervention between the staff members. In my experience, this is quite rare. In over a quarter century of education, I have only had to do this a handful of times.

When two staff members are at the root of a conflict, it can be tempting to pull them into the office and hash it out. This is risky. Only as a last resort would I call the two disgruntled staff members together and appoint myself a formal mediator. In using such an approach, the implication is that I am the judge, and I will listen to both the plaintiff and the defendant and then issue a ruling. I've tried this form of mediation before, but it rarely goes well. I recall a situation in which two teachers were in conflict about a professional development requirement. One teacher, whom I'll call R, was technically the team leader but didn't have any supervisory power over the other teacher, whom I'll call S. Their discord was well known in our building, and I'd grown sick of hearing rumblings about it. In frustration, I called a meeting for after school one day. Apparently, the day of the meeting, R asked one of our building's union representatives to come to the meeting to support her; when S caught wind of this, she asked the building's other union representative to join *her* in support. I had no idea of this change in plans, so when four people walked into my office and sat across from each other, showdown-style, I was speechless. If I had to do it over again, I would have canceled the meeting right then and there—after all, the teachers' interpersonal issue had little to do with working conditions, so it was inappropriate to include union representation. Having the two union representatives in the room created a literal division of our staff; worse yet, it felt like the teachers had shifted the issue into an evaluation of how I, the principal, would handle the meeting—and if I could not bring them to a peaceful resolution, it would seem I had failed. All of this became clear in hindsight, but at the moment I didn't see a way out, so the meeting proceeded. It was an uncomfortable, awkward conversation in which the two union representatives sat quietly, uncertain of their role, and I found myself talking in circles. It was a position I was not prepared to manage well. When we left the meeting, we were no closer to a resolution than we'd been earlier; in fact, our school's culture took a hit because other staff members aligned with either R or S.

Instead of face-to-face mediated interventions, I prefer to talk separately to each person. I might ask to go back and review what happened to lead to this impasse. I ask for help in anticipating future problems by envisioning how each person sees the conflict proceeding. We might discuss potential future manifestations and measure how big the problem is for our school community. I ask each person how they are feeling and if they see potential resolutions. I am careful to avoid swooping in to fix it and rather empower the teacher to consider their role. "What steps can you take toward a resolution?"

When working through staff conflict, there are a few other things to keep in mind.

It's Not About Winning

Even if it seems one teacher is completely out of line and another is an innocent bystander who was caught up in something they could not control, principals should avoid thinking in terms of a clear "right" and "wrong." All teachers bring underlying personal and professional weaknesses, and it's a mistake to choose a side or imply a winner or loser. It might feel like a clean resolution, but the "loser" will never forget.

Avoid Reprimands and Hard Lines

Adults rarely respond well to a scolding or an ultimatum. We may need to say hard things, but we can say them with care and convocation. "I never want to hear about this again" can be framed as "I hope we've come to a long-term solution." The words "You were out of line" may need to be said as "Your actions do not reflect who you are or what we are trying to do here at this school." A threatening "I never want to hear about an angry outburst again" can be said as "It is the expectation that we treat one another with kindness and respect. If you are feeling anger, what might you do to avoid repeating this situation?"

Provide Grace

It helps to remember that collegial discord is as old as time, and it will continue into the infinite future. Concerns and worries outside school absolutely play a part in how teachers interact with one another, and with the increasing pressure faced by teachers today, many of them live with constant low-grade stress every moment they are at work. Staff members who snip at one another might be bending under the pressure. Acknowledging this is a great first step. "I know I've been feeling my stress mount and my emotions fray, so I assume the same is true for you. This is a difficult job, and I want to acknowledge how hard you are working each and every day." This type of opening, differentiated to the setting and situation of your school, will communicate your empathy and recognize the stress that is feeding the conflict.

Excuse or Explanation?

When teachers are in conflict, it helps to understand and acknowledge the "why." Years ago, I heard someone say, "I'd like to tell you why I acted as I did. This isn't an excuse; it's an explanation." I've used that phrase hundreds of times since. Excuses and explanations are very different. Excuses ask for a pass—for a quick, unquestioned forgiveness. Explanations simply provide reasons and background. When leading adults through conflict, explanations help. Excuses don't.

Take Care

I had a mentor once tell me, "Humans have so many frailties." It stuck with me. We all have vulnerabilities and weaknesses, and they might come with buttons or triggers. Others might hit those buttons without even knowing they've done it. We never know what burdens, anxieties, and challenges someone else is facing, so I try to remind myself there is likely more going on beneath the surface—things I might not even consider. Problems with someone's health, home, relationships, children, pets, finances, or mental health are just a few factors. It helps to know frailties exist and offer care, dignity, and respect.

Find Common Ground

When conflict arises between teachers, I like to look for things that are *not* at issue. What is it the teachers do agree on? Are they trying to achieve the same goal but approaching it in the opposite direction? Finding some consensus is a great step going forward. Often, I find teachers agree that they are both trying their best, that there is no ill intent or attempt at harm, and, ironically, that they truly dislike being in conflict with one another. These are small but mighty commonalities and can be used as the first step in moving toward resolution.

Know When to Draw a Hard Line

Even with these considerations, there is one thing you cannot allow: a teacher who acts in an unprofessional, mean, or damaging way. Nothing will hurt your school's professional identity more than allowing one teacher to bully or attack others. As mentioned above, if a teacher is criticizing colleagues, creating divisions, and stirring up conflict, you will need to step in. This takes courage, but as with most courageous leadership decisions, the hard things are the worthy things. You'll never want to lower your expectations out of fear that you won't be liked. The respect you gain from those who are watching from afar is well worth the temporary discomfort of addressing a problematic staff member.

As we wrap up this chapter, I am reminded of the most difficult staff conflict I've ever encountered. It happened years ago. The circumstances were tragic and complicated. A teacher, whom I'll call Ashley, had been fighting breast cancer for years. She was quite ill, and the entire school community rallied around her. Meals were made, visits were scheduled, and her husband and children were supported by our entire school community. Sadly, tragically, she passed away. Our entire school community was wracked with grief. The memorial service was packed with her colleagues and friends. Just months later, whispers began to be heard about another teacher in the building, whom I'll call Lilly. It seemed Lilly had begun to date Ashley's widower. He and Lilly very quickly married, blending their families just months after Ashley's death.

Teachers loyal to Ashley were furious. They iced Lilly out of all staff conversations and activities, refusing to speak to her or even acknowledge her presence. They felt Lilly had taken advantage of a grieving widower and his children. "She stomped on Ashley's grave," I overheard someone say. But Lilly had a few loyal friends who saw it differently.

Ashley's widower had found love again. The children had a stepparent. Love had won. What was the problem?

The entire experience was fraught with feelings and frustration, grief and mourning, resentment and accusations. Everyone had an opinion, each driven by the most intense of human emotions. Many staff looked at me for direction and resolution, but I felt there was little I could do. I listened and tried to offer each side an alternate perspective, but I was careful not to develop an opinion of my own. I knew decisions teachers make about their families in a personal context were not my business, and to my knowledge, students were not having a negative learning experience because of this situation.

But it just wouldn't go away. Months after the marriage, I recognized our school's culture was permanently fractured. Using the anticipate-analyze-act process, I admitted to myself that I'd not been able to anticipate the situation—or how harmful it would be on our staff culture—but I could still analyze and act. I thought carefully about what had happened and how we could fix it. After checking with our HR department, who oversaw staff transfers between schools, I asked Lilly if she wanted to consider a position in a different school in our district, suggesting a new placement might provide a more peaceful working environment. She was understandably upset; why, she wondered, did she have to leave? She'd done nothing wrong. I had a great deal of empathy for her, knowing how difficult it had been for her to work in a place she was disliked so openly. I made sure she understood that a transfer was an option rather than a mandate; it was her choice to make, and I supported her decision either way. She thought about it for several weeks then came to me and admitted that the current situation was too stressful to continue as it was. She agreed to try a new setting. It wasn't a perfect solution—indeed, in some ways, it just moved the problem, because teachers at the new school knew a bit about the situation. Fortunately, though, because the new staff hadn't known Ashley personally, there wasn't the emotional weight of her death to complicate things. In time, Lilly found a positive environment in her new school, and everything settled down.

I recognize many principals do not have the option of transfer, especially those without multiple schools that provide a reassignment system. But big, heavy, emotion-laced conflicts do require outside-the-box thinking, which might involve a change of environment—even if that change is internal. They also require care, compassion, and empathy. Most of all, they require time—the greatest healer of staff conflict.

Let's move away from adults for a bit and spend the next chapter thinking about the conflicts students encounter and how we can provide support in working through them.

6

Conflicts Between Students

Regardless of age, students get into conflict all the time—silent struggles, little skirmishes, big fights, and everything in between. It can be as simple as a brief disagreement between friends, managed with a quick apology. Unfortunately, as we all know, student conflict can get quite a bit more layered and complicated. There may be multiple students involved. There can be spillover issues from incidents that occurred outside the school day. It is rare that student discord exists in isolation, as frequently there are parents, friends, coaches, and community members involved, complicating the situation. Often, the older the students get, the more details and difficulties there are to unravel.

There has been a lot written about strategies schools should use to manage student conflict, and it has taken on many names: discipline, consequences, restorative discipline, positive behavior support structures, and more. Educators are always seeking to find balance between teaching academically rigorous content and managing the predictable disruptions that come from student conflict.

The need for support and expertise is evidenced in the existence of countless vendor-based businesses that sell structures and training to manage student conflict and behavior—some at a high financial price tag. Why so many? Well, likely because so many schools look for help in this area. For one, teachers and principals are on a wide spectrum of experience, confidence, and skill in addressing student conflict. Second, there are innumerable factors that play into why students are in conflict, many out of sight or out of our control. Third, there are wide variations in the climate and culture of a classroom, a school, and a community— variations that have significant effects on how students interact and how teachers respond. We can count on students being in conflict with one another, but we cannot assume there are simple reasons for the conflict, nor can we assume the student knows how to avoid conflict or manage it when it arises. All of these factors can make the job of managing student conflict seem overwhelming.

The best—and most challenging—thing about working with young people is how much they still have to learn about working, collaborating, disagreeing, supporting, and coexisting with other people. There is opportunity in every conflict they face. In providing the appropriate help and support, we can give students the places and spaces to resolve conflict using strategies they will need as adults.

In this chapter, we will dive into some of the ways to manage conflict between students. As we do, the issue of parent involvement is always something to be considered. Even in schools with low parent engagement, the home environment affects how students interact with one another. Indeed, an entire book could be written solely about engaging with parents whose children have faced a social or behavioral challenge at school. Even this chapter about students could quickly be overtaken by considering how to handle parents whose children are in conflict. In other words, there are two things at play here: We know the real power in managing conflict between students lies with the students themselves; however, we can't dismiss the parent component, as it has too much power and influence on the outcome to ignore. For that reason, the first part of this chapter will focus on the strategies and supports we can utilize to help students, and the second part will delve into how to best manage the challenges that come with parents' contribution to student conflict. We will never be able to cover all the possible outcomes and ramifications, but we will consider some of the more common effects of parent involvement and, as in other chapters and sections, will cover some common missteps related to managing parents' role and influence on student conflicts.

Let's start with why student conflict is not something to dread or fear.

Student Conflict: The Chance to Teach

I welcome student conflict because I see it as an opportunity for learning. We all have our own memories of times we learned something important about friendship, social choices, and being part of conflict. When I was in 3rd grade, I passed a note to my very best friend, Tammy, who was, I suspected, changing her allegiance to me and choosing another best friend—a new student named Rose. In my note, I said something nasty and untrue about Rose. Even as I did it, I knew it was wrong. My intention was to provoke a fight between Tammy and Rose and then, I hoped, stand by innocently while Tammy realized it was *me* to whom she should remain loyal. But my teacher intercepted the note. I was mortified. She read it, folded it, and put it in the pocket of her cardigan. Then she quietly went back to working with a small group of students. I waited for my world to end.

When my teacher dismissed the class for lunch, she asked me to stay. I felt the dread of being in big trouble. I felt terrible for disappointing my beloved teacher. Worst of all, Tammy was probably having lunch with Rose.

But my teacher handled it masterfully. "Let's have lunch together," she said. As we ate, she talked to me about friendship, about gossip, about being true to myself and good to others. It provided the opportunity for me to open up to her. I told her I thought my most important friendship was slipping away. Using words and concepts appropriate for an eight-year-old, the teacher helped me think about intentions, long-term outcomes, and ongoing damage I could do by being sneaky and mean. She also pointed out that the note wasn't an indication that I was a bad person—it was just a bad choice. I would recover, she said, and I'd do it by building on my friendships rather than destroying those of other people. Although I would go on to make many more social missteps in my life, the learning that happened in a 3rd grade classroom that day was, quite literally, life changing. It was a crossroad moment, one in which I saw two paths: be a mean girl who provoked problems for others ... or don't. My teacher helped me choose.

Exactly how we can use student conflict as an opportunity to teach depends on the situation. It is sometimes active instruction, such as happened with my 3rd grade teacher, in which there is a conflict—or a potential conflict, in this case—and it receives timely, focused adult intervention. Other times, the instruction is deliberately passive, such as when students experience conflict and teachers stand outside the conversation and let them work it out. More often than we know, it is unintentionally passive, such as when students face conflict and keep the entire situation away from adults. I am always proud of students who work through conflict without asking for help, in exactly the same way I am proud when they *do* ask. Learning which path to take is a sign of maturity—we want our students to be able to assess a situation and decide whether it is something they can manage on their own or whether they need help from an adult.

Teaching through conflict happens all the time, even when the conflict is so significant it rises to the point of behavior intervention or discipline. Discipline's root word comes from *disciplina,* meaning "instruction given, teaching, learning, knowledge," and it is given to *disciplulus,* meaning "pupil, student, follower." To teach a student how to navigate challenges with others is the whole point of doing what we do— more important, I would argue, than the academic content we teach. No one will live a conflict-free life, so developing an extensive toolkit of management skills is an important gift to our students, more effective than making them masters of our subject areas.

Of course, students acquire some of these tools at home, but as we all know, there are limitations to the home setting. It doesn't necessarily hold all the conflict triggers present in a school setting, nor does it mimic the complicated social landscape at school and, eventually, the adult workplace environment our students will enter. Schools and classrooms are living, breathing representations of our larger world—big groups of people, age-level peers, deadlines, competition, politics, distrust, friend-ships, feelings, bad days, good days, and more.

The home setting can be a supportive instructional space where children are appropriately guided through conflict. Yet, as we all know, it can also be the opposite—a place where students see and are even encouraged to manage conflict in negative ways. We've all had the parent announce, "I've told my child that if something happens with another kid, they should just hit them." When school leaders try to counter this approach, reminding students and parents that physical assault is never a solution, we can be dismissed or ignored. That's why we must "teach around" unproductive approaches that are taught in the home. Think of it like reprogramming flawed thinking. If students come to conflict with particular programming—yelling, hitting, throwing, isolating, gossiping, disrupting—we have to reprogram their approach by providing a more effective one. Teachers, principals, counselors, and school staff do this all the time in big and small ways. All teachers—and especially those who work with students struggling with significant behaviors—have an array of tools to try, starting with calming techniques and moving all the way to fully reprogramming actions. Later in this chapter, we'll talk through some effective processes and will identify experts who might help navigate student conflict. For now, though, let's consider why—and how—principals can make teachers the main conduits in managing conflict between students.

Teachers Running Point

Principals simply don't have the time to intervene in all student conflicts. In my conversations with principals, I find the most overwhelmed, overworked, and pessimistic ones are those who are absorbing every disagreement, every argument, and every incident that occurs between students. When there is a problem, it is immediately sent to the office. Instead of being an instructional leader, principals of these schools are in constant triage. That's why the best move principals can make is to empower their staff to be the main point of contact, management, and resolution when students aren't getting along with one another.

Why? Well, teachers are the main point of influence with students. They know them best. Except in rare cases, principals don't have a teacher's depth of knowledge of each student's personality, background, and social capability. That's why principals should serve in a consulting role—always available to talk through a situation, to suggest action steps, to provide perspective and a good pep talk—but not the one to swoop in and take the problem away.

At times, for me, it has taken self-discipline to do this. I like being a fixer and a helper. It's easy to say, "If you have a problem, send the students to me. I'll handle it." But if I take this approach, I'm only providing short-term relief for the teacher and temporarily solving the problem. I am reducing the teacher's ability, power, and confidence by assuming I am better equipped to manage the situation. And I am increasing the likelihood that I will need to take on the next conflict, too, because I made it too easy for the teacher to outsource the solution. When I make an effort to keep the problem in the teacher's hands, I am empowering them by staying behind the scenes with helpful structures and support. But how does this look in action?

When a teacher comes to talk through a conflict simmering between two students, I take care to say things like "How much do you know about the conflict? How do you feel your planned intervention will help? What concerns do you have about the phone call you'll make to the parents?" I don't diagnose; I don't intervene; I don't make the phone call. I just talk it through using "you"—the teacher—as the one who will be taking action.

Here are a few additional questions to guide principals as they help teachers run point on student conflict. These questions are rooted in the process we outlined in Chapter 4 and can be adapted for the individual teacher, the students involved, and the hoped-for outcome. The intent is to ask them in a collaborative, curious, helpful mindset rather than to make the teacher feel you are looking to place blame. You'll notice the questions should prompt reflection, ideas, and action from the teacher—not the principal.

Anticipate:

- Were there indications this problem was brewing?
- Did you know about previous incidents between these students?
- When you intervened, what worked and what didn't?
- Have there been similar conflicts with other students?
- Was there a plan in place, either informal or formal, to address conflict in either of these students?

Analyze:

- What did you see and observe during the conflict?
- What do you think will help?
- How can I help you?
- What will help you mediate and resolve the conflict?

Act:

- Before you call the parent, would you like me to help you rehearse some talking points?
- What setting or environment will be best for the students?
- How much time would you like to allot to this process?
- What are some of the details relevant to a successful mediation? Are there any other staff members or resources that would help?
- What structures can you put in place to avoid another event?
- What do you want to do differently?

It goes without saying that there are times principals have to take over student conflict issues, particularly if the conflict leaves others unsafe, is overly time-consuming for the teachers, or is outside the skill or knowledge level of staff. This includes anything on the higher levels of the discipline handbook, anything that requires a thorough investigation, and any repeated offenders with larger schoolwide implications. That's not to say the teacher is no longer involved—they just step back a bit (especially if they have to go back to their classroom to tend to the instruction of the rest of the students). Still, a principal should try to avoid managing the conflict completely alone. I try to keep teachers involved as much as I can because they know the series of antecedents leading to the conflict, and they are the ones who will need to live with any ramifications of the conflict resolution.

Most teachers don't involve the principal in low-level conflicts; they've "got it," so to speak, and are experienced and skillful in handling such situations. Indeed, it's a point of pride for most teachers that they do not need the principal's help very often. Some teachers almost never do. Those are the ones who, when they do come to the principal with a conflict, should probably receive immediate attention. I once worked with a fabulous physical education teacher who, in the 10 years I knew her, did not have a single student issue she brought to me. Not one, in an entire decade. Even in physical education class—a class environment ripe for opportunity for conflict. So when, one late spring day, she brought two students to my office, I dropped everything I was doing and focused completely on her issue; I knew it had to be beyond her scope and she genuinely needed me. It was, she did, and I was more than happy to help her. Later, after everything was resolved, she actually apologized for bothering me. I told her I'd see her in another decade.

Analyze the Situation

When students get embroiled in conflict and it does end up on the principal's plate, the first step is to figure out what really happened. This is where we analyze the situation. Sometimes this is a short and simple conversation between one or two students; other times, it grows into a detailed investigation. In the beginning of my career, I was very anxious when I had to lead a large investigation, and I'd worry constantly about all the ways I could mess it up. But I had the wrong mindset—I was approaching conflict investigation with an emotional, binary lens. I thought there was someone who was right, someone who was wrong, and it was my job to figure out who was on either side of that dichotomy. With time, I've learned it is usually more complex. I find that taking a curious approach works best—almost as if I am researching a mystery. I want to find out facts; I want to figure out what led up to the problem; I want to work toward a fair, equitable outcome; and I want everyone involved to learn something they can apply in future situations.

Let's discuss how to manage a solid investigation. For the purposes of simplicity, this section will focus on steps the principal might take, but hopefully the students' teacher or guidance counselor is working alongside the principal or even doing this investigative work themselves. Let's assume, again for simplicity, that there has been a disagreement between two students that escalated into a physical altercation. The strategies present in this section can be applied to any other issue, though, simply by inserting any relevant details of a specific situation.

Connect with the Teacher

An investigation often starts with knowing what the teacher—or other professional staff—has seen, knows, or understands. What are the facts? What feelings or emotions are relevant? What previous contact or actions have come from the parents?

Connect with the Student

Many principals ask students to write a statement, especially if they are old enough to do so or if there are multiple students involved. Other times, they speak to the student and take detailed notes. It's best when this step occurs with deliberate speed to avoid students getting together to plan a united message that they hope will keep them out of trouble.

Decide Who Else Might Have a Helpful Perspective

Sometimes talking to one student reveals the need to dig deeper and talk to other students. As noted above, students communicate with one another very, very quickly, so adding more student perspective must be done with care, knowing student conversations won't be insulated from one another.

Connect with Others Involved

This might include other students who saw what happened, teachers who anticipated the conflict or tried previous interventions, or staff members who work closely with these particular students, even in unrelated or unstructured environments.

View Cameras

Years ago, I was resistant to the concept of using cameras for investigations, because I disliked the idea of constant surveillance. I thought it would oppress natural human behavior. I have done a 180-degree philosophical turn on this. Having investigated conflict in schools with no cameras and in schools with multiple, I can say with no hesitation that camera footage is a gift when there are conflicting accounts of a physical altercation, a theft, student movement and location, or unsafe behavior choices. These days, cameras are everywhere, even on many front porches. They have become permissible—even expected—in places in which there is no expectation of privacy—like schools. My husband works in a relatively new school building. When it was built, it was equipped with cameras in every hall and common area. He says it has drastically cut down on investigation time and allows principals to start at the end of the story—a fight, a shove, a trip, a theft, an argument—rather than try to gather various accounts and reconstruct it from the beginning. Starting at the end reverses the process, working backward toward antecedents. In other words, camera footage allows us to spend less time trying to figure out *what* happened and more time trying to figure out *why* it happened.

Know Your Stuff

Following the law and adhering to district policy is essential in investigating and reacting to a conflict situation. Since 1975, when it was decided by the U.S. Supreme Court that students have property and liberty rights during an investigation, the law has been clear on requirements of a student investigation. The case, *Goss v. Lopez,* 419 U.S. 565, involved nine students in Columbus, Ohio, who were given a 10-day suspension without first having a hearing. The court determined that students must be given notice of allegations, an explanation of why the allegations were made, and the chance to present their version of the events (Justia Law, n.d.). Beyond this due process requirement, another consideration is a district's policy manual. Many principals don't know where to find, how to read, and how to implement their own district policies. I, too, wasn't familiar with policy until I made the connection between our student handbook—of which I was very familiar—and the district policy. When I began studying policy and accompanying guidelines, I understood they are developed and written by school law experts and then approved by boards of education. They are the best protection that principals have against parent pushback and legal missteps. Principals do not need to be an expert on every policy; they just need to know where to find, read, and use them.

Ask Questions

When analyzing a conflict, it's hard to know what someone else was thinking or why they made certain decisions—especially a child. Asking a lot of questions helps because it can clarify the child's intent and purpose. It will tease out any dishonesty, background information, or allegiances between students. The more questions you ask, the clearer the picture becomes. Rather than take on the tone of an interrogation, these questions should be asked out of a genuine curiosity and intent to understand.

- Can you tell me more about that?
- What happened next?
- What were you thinking about as the incident was happening?
- I'm not sure I understand. Can you say it again? Or maybe tell me in a different way?
- How do you feel about what happened?
- How do you see this incident ending?

When asked in a conversational and nonthreatening way, prompts like these will guide the conversation to be informative and insightful.

Listen

After taking part in dozens of investigations, as many principals have, it can begin to feel mundane and repetitive. You may even assume, early in the investigation, that you already know how the sequence of events played out—you have seen it all before, right? But even in situations that feel routine, there might be a detail to be uncovered that has big implications. Moreover, there is always a child, no matter what age, who could be in a significant crisis because of the conflict. The best tool to ward off complacency is active listening. Disciplining ourselves to listen and piece together the full story will help us honor the emotional distress of anyone involved; it will also help us determine how to proceed with next steps.

Act

Make a Plan

Once you feel like you have all relevant and accurate details, you'll want to make a plan to move forward. This will involve outlining responsibilities of students and staff, making any adjustments to schedule or class environment, and making a decision about restorative action, consequences, or discipline.

Communicate

Of all the things I know about conflict between students, I know this: In the absence of clear and correct information, people—students, teachers, and parents—will create their own story about what happened. Informing stakeholders with the most thorough and accurate information, within the bounds of what you can share with them, will reduce criticism and false narratives.

Help Students with a Communication Plan

Students are especially vulnerable to the stories other people create about them, and I try to always remember what it feels like to be young, insecure, and uncertain about how to talk about a conflict after it's over. The gossip and interrogation by peers can seem truly overwhelming to a child or teenager. I have addressed this by coaching students on what they can say. Even something as small as pulling them out of class for a few quick questions can have repercussions—when they return to class, they might get peppered with questions from classmates, putting them in an uncomfortable position. To deal with it, they may try to lie or deflect, which could make the problem worse. In an effort to help avoid this problem, I will ask students if they feel anxious about what to say to their classmates, and then I'll provide suggestions. We might even rehearse what they might say and how they will say it. Several years ago, I did this with a student after she'd had a big run-in with one of the girls on her team, and we both felt good about her preparedness. As she left, she admitted she was still nervous about the cafeteria. She knew friends would press her for details she wasn't willing to share. We talked about a few things she could say. None felt right, so I suggested she just ask to not discuss it. "They'll never accept that," she said. "Well, I think you should just roll your eyes and say, 'Whatever.' Then go about your day," I suggested. The student stared at me. "I've never heard an adult tell me I could say, 'Whatever.' I've *really* never had an adult tell me to roll my eyes." We had a good laugh, and she went to lunch with a smile.

A Note on Social Media

Not long ago, I had lunch with a middle school principal friend. As we sat down, I asked her how her school year was going so far. Her eyes filled with tears. "Social media is ruining my professional happiness," she said. "Dealing with its repercussions has become all I do."

Disruptions stemming from social media have taken over the time of teachers, principals, and guidance counselors. Social media interactions cause constant friction between students, and the issue gets more complicated when parents get involved. Cases involving bullying, threats to school safety, slander of school officials, and academic cheating or plagiarism have no end with the constant presence of social media and the unrelenting accessibility of internet connection. In early 2023, the Seattle Public Schools filed a lawsuit against large social media platforms alleging that their targeted marketing of young people was directly causing problems with social-emotional wellness, thereby creating a financial and educational burden on school districts (Merod, 2023). As of this writing, there was no resolution to that lawsuit, but it does reflect the frustration and helplessness school officials feel when trying to manage the damage done by student use of social media.

So, what's a principal to do? First, there is great value in being proactive. Open, honest dialogue with parents, both before school starts and throughout the year, can keep parents aware of the repercussions and risks of social media. Most parents don't know how often their children are on their phones, and most assume their child would not say unkind, cruel, or dangerous things on social media. Most parents do not even know the availability of some apps or what their intended audience and outcome are. I encourage principals to take a lead role in educating parents. I once led a training for parents titled "'No' Is a Complete Sentence." It was extremely highly attended, as parents were eager for guidance and insight on how to restrict and manage their child's use of technology.

The second action steps principals might take is having a voice in developing school or district guidelines regarding social media. In recent years, some schools have taken the step to ban or significantly limit cell phone usage during the day—a move that takes courage to uphold when parents push back. Others hesitate to fully restrict phone usage, instead creating time windows or zones within the school in which phones can be used. This won't alleviate the social media usage outside school, but it might help manage the ongoing onslaught of social media repercussions, at least during the day.

Third, principals can keep an eye on legal decisions that may have an effect on how districts can respond to social media. A 2021 U.S. Supreme Court case, *Mahanoy Area School District v. B.L.,* found districts cannot regulate speech that takes place off campus and after school hours if it does not include threats or bullying. Applauded by some administrators and bemoaned by others, the decision clarified that schools do not have full reach to regulate or discipline students for posts and responses. Of course, in most cases, it is irrelevant to principals whether the speech should be regulated, because the bottom line is this: If a social media post disrupts the day, it needs to be addressed one way or another—through discipline, perhaps, but more likely through communication with parents, students, or teachers or through social-emotional support. Every case is different; the details are different. If it disrupts learning, it is something that will need to be handled.

Build a Team

Earlier in this chapter, we discussed the toolkit needed to help students navigate conflict, and we've discussed the role teachers should take. As we have noted, it is best for principals to empower teachers to respond to student conflicts, following an anticipate-analyze-act process. Teachers work hard to build trust with their students so they are best equipped to anticipate potential conflict, gather details to respond, and then develop a plan to mediate or resolve it. We've also acknowledged that conflicts between students sometimes escalate beyond what a teacher can or should handle. The conflict might be beyond their skill, training, or comfort level—or they simply can't get to it because of instructional responsibilities. The dual responsibility of teaching academic content while managing disruptive student conflicts is often unmanageable, which is why principals might need to intervene.

Principals have knowledge of school policy, can conduct a wider investigation, and can shift their day's priorities more easily than a teacher can. There are limitations, though; for example, many times principals find themselves in a counseling role, which can feel off-kilter without specific training on counseling students.

That's why principals benefit if they "build a bench" of people who can help anticipate, analyze, and act in conflict situations. It takes pressure off the principal while also providing important balanced perspectives in supporting students. Let's take a look at other professionals who can come to the table to work through conflicts with students.

RTI and MTSS Coordinators

If your school has someone who oversees interventions and programs, such as a Response to Intervention (RTI) or Multi-Tiered Systems of Support (MTSS) coordinator, they might be the liaison you need to gather expertise and ideas together. MTSS coordinators can build a bridge among students, teachers, administration, and parents—and they can keep track of relevant data that will guide future decision making.

Counselors

School counselors do a fabulous job managing student conflict. The very best ones are truly inspiring. The best example of this was a counselor I worked with for six years. Watching him work felt like getting a free graduate-level class in counseling, human behavior, and child psychology. He was unflappable, calm at all times, and one of the best listeners I've ever encountered. He avoided judgment and kept his eye on the goal to give the student a voice, provide perspective, offer options for resolution, and have the student learn important lifelong strategies through social interaction. Under his watch, conflict between students certainly happened, but it never escalated beyond a reasonable scope. He helped set a school climate of calm acceptance.

But many schools don't have the gift of a skilled counselor. Last summer, I worked with a school district that was struggling with ongoing student conflicts that were, many times, turning into larger issues of discipline and parent involvement. When I found out the district only had two counselors, assigned to five different buildings, I knew I'd identified the problem. The counselors were spread so thin they spent the majority of their time on legitimate crisis situations, leaving only a couple hours a week at each school doing proactive guidance work. It's impossible to put in a schoolwide climate of instruction, support, and intervention with such limited support.

The American School Counselor Association has recommended a student-to-counselor ratio of 250:1, but these numbers are simply a starting point; the age of students, the responsibilities on the counselors, equity and socioeconomic factors, and school staffing allocations all affect these ratios. Because counselors often have college and career readiness responsibilities at the high school level, high schools have a national average range of student-to-counselor ratio between 204:1 and 243:1. Surprisingly, and unacceptably, the national average ratio range at grades K–8 is 613:1 to 787:1 (National Center for Education Statistics, n.d.). With numbers this high for young students who have much to learn about navigating conflict, it's no wonder teachers and principals feel overwhelmed. Indeed, I've heard many principals say they spend most of their day doing counselor-type work. These numbers show why. If a principal has any opportunity to advocate for additional support, they might want to use that power to advocate for more counselors.

Social Workers

School-based social work is a growing field. So is social work itself. According to the *Occupational Outlook Handbook* by the U.S. Bureau of Labor Statistics (2022), social work was projected to grow 9 percent by 2031, faster than any other occupation. Yet, as we all know, social work is a poorly paid field with a massive workload and a system that often works against the very people it wants to help. Moreover, school-based social work requires specific skills, the same skills educators have mastered, so I believe we need to think outside the box to better support our schools in how they help students by adding social workers to our schools. My superintendent, Dr. John Marschhausen, has been a trailblazer in this area. I watched, dubious at first but then thrilled, as he reacted to a dire need for more student support by looking to the field of social work. Using federal dollars allocated from COVID relief funds, he developed a partnership with a local university to train existing, mid-career teachers in a master's degree in social work. These teachers, upon completion of their training, were given positions in the district—on their existing place on the salary scale, with the same benefits and contribution to their teacher's state retirement system. This was the most masterful, creative, and intuitive response to a problem I have ever seen. By the time this book is published, all of my district's 25 schools will have a guidance counselor and a social worker in each building. These social workers will have the training and certification to expand their scope beyond school counseling to do school-based family outreach, work flexible hours that meet the needs of parents and children, and connect us with social services to better help families. By collaborating with teachers, principals, and their school's guidance counselor, this school-based social worker will be a crucial connector between school and family, working to alleviate some of the hidden issues that manifest themselves in conflict at school.

Behavior Analysts

There is never one clear reason why a student struggles with significant behavior problems, because the "why" is so varied. It could be a biological or chemical imbalance, early trauma, PTSD, anxiety, stress, or a home environment that encourages or rewards conflict. Or it could just be a culmination of events on a very bad day. Understanding all the antecedents takes a skilled eye, which is why I am always thrilled to hear about districts that dedicate specially trained staff members to help. Districts that have hired behavior specialists are doing their teachers an enormous favor—oftentimes, the expertise of a trained behavior specialist is just what is needed for resolution.

Language Experts

Communication is crucial in understanding conflict and its resolution. Unfortunately, many times, and for many various reasons, young people struggle to communicate. Whether it is a communication barrier related to a native language, the young age of a child, or a situation in which a language disability might impede clear communication, there are experts who can help ensure it's not a language problem impeding a conflict's resolution. An English language teacher, an interpreter, a translator, or a speech-language pathologist might have insight to help work through a student conflict.

Common Missteps with Student Conflict

Now that we have discussed how to use student conflict as a teaching tool, how to empower teachers to manage student conflicts, how to run a solid investigation, and what experts to rely upon, let's talk about some common missteps principals make in managing student conflict. There are several things to avoid, including relying on limited information, intervening too soon, being too involved or not involved enough, and taking student conflicts as a reflection of your professional or personal success. Let's take a look at each one individually.

Relying on Limited Situational Evidence

I've been known to be impulsive and move too quickly when trying to resolve conflict. It happens when I take the first version of the story I heard, call a student in, and announce my "findings." This is why an investigation—even a small one—can help avoid problems. It's best to try to get the full, factual story before acting.

Intervening Too Soon

Whenever possible, we should let students work out their conflicts. Intervening too soon sends the message that we don't trust they can do it well. Unless someone is unsafe, it is actually a vote of confidence when we stand back and allow students to mediate and manage their issues.

Becoming Over- or Under-Involved in Creating the Solution

It's not easy to determine just how involved to get in student conflict. There is always a balance between doing all the repair work for the students or allowing them to do it. As with most of what we do with students, using a facilitator mindset is a great way to find that balance. We want to follow the lead of the students as much as possible, listening to their needs to determine the appropriate level of adult intervention. We can suggest, prompt, support, and guide—but we shouldn't take it over unless necessary.

Reacting Personally

We can never assume that a child knows how best to react to a challenging social situation, and thus we shouldn't target our emotions at them when they make poor decisions. Nor should we allow ourselves to "own" the reason they became embroiled in conflict. The existence of conflict isn't a reflection on you as a leader, and it isn't a reflection on your teachers or your school. As mentioned several times in this book, conflict is inevitable and should be viewed as part of what we do—not an indication of our shortcomings.

The Parent Component

Most of the time, I actually enjoy working with students in conflict because I enjoy seeing them learn and grow when they work through disagreements and problems. While adults tend to be set in their ways in how they respond and react to interpersonal interactions, students are more receptive to the input and guidance from teachers and principals.

When students fight—with words or with physical altercations—most principals feel confident intervening toward productive resolution. But there is always an additional layer of conflict facing us: how to communicate the issue with parents so they can support and align with us. As all seasoned principals know, student conflict investigation and resolution can be going quite well—right up to the point of letting the parent know it happened. Then everything gets more complex.

There is no surefire way to handle parents who get involved in student conflict. Parents react in ways that are hard to predict. They carry memories from their own experiences at school, which may be painful or provoke anxiety and cause them to over-advocate for their child, sometimes even in spite of the facts. They may not trust the systems and processes that guide schools, genuinely feeling their child will not get a fair shake unless they intervene. Still, parents are the most important influence in a child's life, and a collaborative relationship is the best way to approach communication with parents.

Conflict and Communication

In my experience, calling parents to report a conflict is sometimes easy and seamless; other times, it can feel like a disaster. There were many times I needed to make a call and knew the parents were not going to take the information well. I would sit in my office, staring at my phone, knowing I had to pick it up and dial, knowing I would likely encounter anger, disbelief, and denial. I would count down from 10, telling myself I'd dial when I got to zero. Then I'd count down again. I hated the way I might be spoken to and hated that parents might get angry at me rather than accept there was a problem to be solved. Bullying issues were the worst ones to try to explain, because *bully* is a heavy, weighted word that triggers many feelings, and it is difficult to prove fault. Many times, I have been personally attacked for my attempt to communicate about one of those situations. I always hoped my approach would be the key to an amicable conversation, but I didn't always get it right. If I had a dollar for every time I misjudged, mishandled, or misunderstood the best way to communicate with a parent about their child's conflict with another student, I'd be a wealthy woman.

Do we need to call parents every time there is an incident? Well, no. Conflicts between students happen hundreds of times a day. Many of these conflicts don't even make it to the principal's desk. At times they don't even make it to the teacher. When they do, the teacher or principal might work through it and consider it too inconsequential to warrant a phone call home.

So what about when the parent calls and wants to discuss an incident that, to you or your staff, felt like a non-issue? They might say, "My child had a problem today, you knew about it, and you didn't even call me?" In those cases, I found it was best to stand by the decision: "The issue was not one that warranted a phone call; it was a common conflict and we resolved it at school. I am so glad your child told you about it, but here at school, we consider the situation over and we're eager to move on." Sometimes parents will insist that going forward, they will be called *anytime* their child is in a conflict. These are rare, so I found it easy to agree to do so, but I would always qualify it with this: "As long as the conflict requires adult intervention, we will call you. If not, we may not even know it occurred. We both need to trust your child can work through typical conflicts on their own."

Of course, proactive communication probably is the best course of action, even if the conflict is small. When contacting parents, I would start by saying, "Today there was an issue between your child and another student, and I am calling to explain what happened and what our resolution will be." It's possible that the conversation will go sideways, with the parent making assumptions without knowing all the information, but if you stick to facts as you know them and remind the parents you are calling to be proactive, you can never be accused of overlooking or ignoring their child's issues.

For bigger problems, it might be better to invite the parent in to discuss the situation. Having the student present might be helpful, as might the presence of a teacher or counselor with knowledge of the situation. Again, these conversations should not be accusatory or emotional; they should rely on facts and take on a calm, reassuring, and collaborative tone.

Even with this guidance, there will still be times when communication with parents is ineffective. Let's think about a few ways we might make a communication error—and how to avoid it.

Common Missteps with Parents

Being Intimidated

Some parents consider conversations with the principal about their children to be a power struggle. They might try to out-power you by sharing their job title, qualifications, and experiences. They may raise their voice or use aggressive language. They may bring additional people to a meeting. Attempts to intimidate you may or may not be intentional, but digging deep to find confidence and conviction will serve you well. I believe inexperienced, young, female, or minoritized administrators are especially susceptible to this. My first year as a principal, I was 29 years old and still learning. I had a parent approach me at an athletic contest to challenge me about an incident that had occurred days earlier. He raised his voice, postured his body, and wildly gestured in my face as he outlined how incompetent I was. He cursed and called me names. Although my heart was racing, I remained calm and nonreactive. An older, taller male colleague was standing next to me and witnessed the whole thing, including my attempts to deescalate the situation. He stared at me, shocked, after the parent had left. "I have *never* been spoken to that way," he admitted. "I have a whole new admiration for young women in this role." I have been treated terribly as an administrator, although incidents of this nature have definitely lessened as I aged—perhaps because I am no longer younger than the parents in my school, but also perhaps because I am more confident and experienced. Confidence brought an important gift—the refusal to let myself be intimidated or bullied by parents.

Refusing to Communicate

I once worked in a school in which one particular parent, whose child was often in conflict, would regularly show up at school in the morning and demand a meeting. One of my colleagues encouraged me to refuse to meet with them or call the police if they showed up. I am glad I never took this advice. Instead, I set boundaries. I wouldn't necessarily drop everything to meet with them right away—I'd ask them to come back in an hour or two or invite them to wait until I could wrap up my immediate commitments—but I would not turn them away. In time, I was able to convince them that dropping in only slowed the process, because there was no way I could speak to a situation for which I had no knowledge. Finally, they began to call and make an appointment first, which gave me time to prepare for our conversation.

Taking It Personally

I have a friend, Dr. Dustin Miller, a professor at Ohio State University who teaches aspiring principals and superintendents. He often reminds them, "They are not mad at you. They are mad at your title." Since you are the principal, you are the recipient of a parent's feelings and frustrations that arise when their child is involved in conflict. A good trick is to try to imagine a different principal approached by a parent as they stand in the office, talk on the phone, or work in the car pickup line. In playing out the imaginary scenario, it's easy to see the imaginary principals having the same anger directed toward them. It's not you—it's the job you have.

Acquiescence

It's perfectly OK to change course during a student conflict because you receive updated information or find out additional details. It's rarely a good idea to change course because a parent told you to. If a parent contests a decision you've made and you give in to their demands, word will spread that you . . . well, that you give in to parental demands. Although it takes courage, it's best to stick to what you know is the right course of action.

Attempting to Mediate Between Families

When students find themselves in conflict that appears unresolvable, there are times parents will ask school officials to stage a mediation between families. This is generally a very bad idea. Both parties will feel they are going to court to plead their case and will want the teacher or administrator to choose sides and announce a winner.

The first time I was asked to mediate between families, I didn't know what to say. Two middle school girls had a fight, and both girls fiercely believed they had been wronged by the other. For weeks prior to the fight, they'd been calling one another names, challenging one another online, and had developed a deep bench of classmates on their respective side. The fight was brief but extremely disruptive. I investigated the situation, determined they were equally at fault, removed both girls, and planned for a transition back to school with the guidance counselor. The plan included work with each individual girl and, ultimately, time with them together in the counselor's office to discuss how they could peacefully coexist. Then my phone started to ring. The parents and stepparents of both girls, all of whom lived in a nearby apartment complex, were insisting that I hold a meeting—with all of us. They wanted a mediation, with me in the middle, to discuss the girls' fights, their history of friendship and conflict, and get it all out in the open. Both sides, separately, insisted they deserved an apology from the other girl.

I called a colleague and asked what I should do.

"No matter what, do *not* host a family intervention," my friend wisely advised. "How the families interact is not your problem. The only thing you need to be concerned about is how the students feel and perform when they are at school. What happens in the neighborhood is not only out of the scope of your work—it is out of your control too. Focus on the students and let the adults do what they will do." I have held on to these words for years and have become more convinced of their truth. I have colleagues who have tried to mediate between families, and they always admit their attempts just made the situation worse—their words were repeated out of context, their mediation options were not embraced by both parties, and their resolutions were used against them in later conflicts.

When refusing to stage family interventions, I have been asked, "Why not? Wouldn't getting everyone in a room together be the best course of action?" Rather than go into the multiple reasons for the denial, I'll just say, "Family mediation is not what we do." It's true. As a school principal, my ultimate goal is to support students. I need to mediate between students, not become a player in family or neighborhood conflicts.

Although this chapter has extensively covered some of the interventions we can provide for student conflicts, it's important to remember there is no magic potion to ensure successful mediation every time. With confidence and practice, though, principals can grow very skilled at helping students work through their disagreements and teaching them how to make conflict resolution a lifelong skill.

Some of the tools we discussed about communicating with parents will reappear in our next chapter, when we consider how to best manage conflict between teachers and parents.

7

Conflicts Between Staff and Parents

Let's begin this chapter by acknowledging the wide variances in how parents view schools. The school-to-parent relationship appears simple but is, in fact, layered in complexity. Since every parent was once a child who attended school, they all have memories that form their assumptions and expectations of the school experience. Parents love their children in a way no one else can understand, and as such, they do everything they can to protect and advocate for them. Ideally, a parent thinks of the school as a trusted partner in education. Unfortunately, and increasingly, there are parents who see schools as an adversary or threat.

As schools are asked to take on more and more responsibilities, especially related to behavior and wellness, it is ironic that these additional responsibilities are accompanied by resistance—not from all parents, of course, but certainly from specific groups who are suspicious of the overall intentions of educators. Personally, I have found this to be disheartening, but I have tried to frame it as an opportunity to improve how my staff and I interact with parents.

History provides a fascinating story of the evolution of parent input in schools. In my dissertation research with Ohio State University, I studied the path of education in the United States from the 1600s to today.

The nation's earliest schools did not have principals or superintendents, governed instead by local councils of civic and business leaders. Teachers worked in small schools or one-room classrooms, and they had the ultimate say in the education and discipline of all students. Parent input was not welcomed. Strict behavior expectations were reinforced both at school and at home. Poorly paid and with scant training, teachers were free to rule over their classrooms as they chose. For several hundred years, they had limited oversight or accountability.

In the 19th century, the country's population growth, with a corresponding increase in student enrollment, created a need for a lead teacher—called a "principal teacher"—who was appointed to oversee multiple classrooms, supervise teachers, and handle behavior and discipline. This principal teacher was almost always male, as women were assumed unable to manage unruly students. Eventually, districts hired principals and superintendents to manage schools, teachers, and students. Rural areas made up most of the student population, and schools were often the hub of a community. In partnership with the local church, schools hosted cultural and holiday events and were seen as the conduit for teaching nationalistic, religious, and moral values to students. Parents were often present for these community-based events but did not have a prominent voice in an individual child's educational process.

Things began to change in the early years of the 20th century. As the governing councils evolved into modern-day school boards, and as school districts grew, parent input increased and evolved toward advocacy for one's own child rather than an automatic alignment with the community school and unquestioned trust in individual teachers.

One of the things I enjoy most about educational leadership is the relationships I have with parents. For both myself and the teachers with whom I work, collaborating with parents can be enjoyable and productive. Connections with parents enrich the entire experience for teachers, students, and the overall school community. Even in situations in which parents are not actively engaged—often due to their overflowing work schedules, transient home situations, or demands on their time— two-way communication and trusting relationships can make powerful bonds between school and home.

Unfortunately, there are a few parents who resist partnership. Some even seem to sabotage efforts from the school. I've often thought how pleasant a principal's job would be if not for the few parents who throw up barriers and complaints with regularity. Indeed, there have been years in which the demands of just a few parents have taken up most of the time I spent interacting with our community. In rare cases, I have lived with constant anxiety because of an abusive, slanderous approach by one or two parents. As stated in Chapter 1, a very small percentage of parents require this intense kind of management—in my anecdotal estimate, it's 1 percent or less. We will discuss how to handle that small percentage later in this chapter.

Fortunately, most parents are not nearly as aggressive or combative as the most problematic parents. The majority are very supportive of teachers and of a school's overall mission. They want a solid and strong relationship with their child's teachers and principal. They want to feel part of a school community. In that sense, the key elements to a positive relationship already exist. The trust and positivity are already in place; they are ours to lose.

And how is it lost? Almost without exception, I find parents lose faith in schools when something has happened to break their trust. For individual teachers and principals, the break might not even be in our control; trust may have been broken long ago, when that parent was a student and something occurred to make them think of the schools as an adversary. Perhaps it happened more recently, though still outside our control—a problem with a previous school, a run-in with a certain teacher, or a media narrative that schools are not to be trusted. And it could have happened within our control, recently, with a student's current classroom situation. For me, the breaks in trust that happen under my watch cut more deeply for two reasons: I wish I could have stopped whatever incident created it, and the parent frustration is fresh and seems to loom over everything. Yet, in some ways, this is a positive thing, because the break can be fixed by the people who broke it.

The steps to managing conflict between staff and parents follow the same process discussed in earlier chapters—anticipate, analyze, and act. As part of the work of anticipating conflict, let's dive a little deeper into the things that can happen to hurt the relationship between teachers and parents.

Common Missteps

Conflicts between staff and parents happen for many reasons. Ironically, many arise from positive intentions, but mistakes or missteps got in the way of the intended outcome. As in other chapters, we will first consider some of these missteps and will then reexamine each one to determine how to avoid them.

Not Listening

Parents feel understandable frustration when they are not heard or when they feel their opinion doesn't matter. Many times, when confronted by parents, teachers dig their heels into "winning" a disagreement. This makes the parent feel that the teacher's mind is made up and there is nothing to be done to change it. When staff refuse to hear and consider the perspective of a parent, tempers flare and reciprocal listening is no longer possible. Communication is a two-way street. If we give information, we need to be willing to receive it back.

Defensiveness

When parents ask questions, teachers sometimes feel they are under attack. I spoke recently to a teacher who was struggling with one of her parents, saying, "Every time she has questions for me, it feels like I'm on trial." When teachers jump too quickly to defend their stance, it makes them appear as if they did do something wrong, and it empowers the parent to keep pushing for a different outcome. Worst of all, like not listening, defensiveness prohibits two-way communication.

Denial

Students sometimes bring home a story to a parent that isn't exactly as it happened or how the teacher saw it. When the parent reaches out to the teacher to explain the child's perspective, it's instinctual to respond with "That's not what happened" or "That's wrong." A blanket denial of the parent's perspective will just create a "he said, she said" argument that is difficult to settle.

False Reassurances

Many teachers, especially inexperienced ones, try to reassure parents with promises and reassurances that aren't true. Not long ago, I worked with a teacher who got anxious whenever a parent expressed concern or worry. She would jump in and say things like "Oh, don't worry! Your daughter is so smart, talented, and popular! She is going to be just fine!" or "It really isn't a big deal! Your son is brilliant, and everyone loves him!" While these things may have been true, they were not contextually appropriate or relevant. To shower a parent with vague compliments may feel good in the moment, but it doesn't provide tangible information or a plan to move forward. Additionally, it sets up future teachers to fail because a parent may not understand the depth of a child's challenges.

Being Too Personal

I once worked with a teacher who tried to connect with parents by constantly talking about her own children. When she had to deliver difficult information about behavior, for example, she would say, "I know how you feel. I have two boys myself, and they are constantly getting in trouble at school." Then she would tell multiple stories about her boys and their challenges. When talking about a student's academic struggles, she would say, "You're not alone. My son has an IEP too. I'll tell you a bit about the things he's working on." She would go so far as to share her son's documents with other parents. Her intention was to try to bond with the parent over a shared journey; she wanted to offer reassurance using her children as an example. Instead, she created frustration. One parent said to me, "We're here to talk about my children—not hers." Parents want to know the focus is on their child and their specific situation.

Quick Fixes

To appease parents who are in conflict with teachers, it's tempting to try to find a quick solution. "I spoke too quickly," a teacher once told me after making promises of time and support she couldn't possibly provide. "The parent was so angry, and I just wanted it to go away." When the promises weren't met, the parent was further frustrated and thought of the teacher as dishonest and incompetent.

Deflecting Blame for Communication Mishaps

As stated earlier, miscommunication is a common thread in conflict between teachers and parents. Many conflicts occur when parents don't have accurate, timely, or thorough information. When this happens, it might be a teacher's instinct to place blame elsewhere by saying, "I'm putting information in a weekly newsletter. It's not my fault she's not reading it," or, "I tried to tell that parent about his son's behaviors, but he chose not to hear me." If no one is receiving information, it's not being communicated well.

Being Reactive

When parents feel they need to fight against the school, it is usually in response to something that has already happened—something they didn't know about, don't understand, or dislike in how it was handled. They get angry and call the school to advocate for a different outcome. Situations like this put parents on the offense and staff on the defense, because responding comes down to two impossible choices: stick to the original outcome no matter what or take the parent's feedback and adjust—which might lead to additional conflicts. Being in a reactionary mode pits staff against parents in two distinct sides.

Reactive responses usually occur because of a breakdown in communication. Although some teachers are excellent communicators, others struggle to keep parents in the loop with what is happening in the classroom, how their child is doing, or if there are issues and concerns. Parents hate to be surprised, especially in situations where there should have been earlier communication. Take, for example, a teacher who contacts a parent about a discipline situation and references several previous incidents. The parent will feel ambushed and rightly wonder, "Why didn't they call me when the problem actually began?" Being in reaction mode reinforces a parent's negative opinion of a school's processes.

Strategies and Options

By simply identifying these common missteps, principals are activating the *anticipate* and *analyze* portion of the process outlined earlier, putting them well on their way to helping teachers avoid and resolve issues with parents. To shift into *action,* let's reconstruct each into a solutions-based response that will be helpful to both the teacher involved in the conflict and the principal who might be intervening. As stated earlier, trust is at the root of many of these solutions and strategies; communication is the way to reinforce that trust. Each strategy outlined here will give a specific action to complete the process.

Let's first put the spotlight on the importance of the teacher—not the principal—as a resolver of conflict. I have known many principals who feel it is their job to protect teachers from parents. This view is problematic for several reasons. First, it encourages a culture in which teachers do not have to build strong relationships with their students' parents. Second, it simply isn't sustainable. A principal has too many responsibilities to be expected to intervene whenever a parent is disgruntled or unhappy. Third, parents will learn to go directly to the principal for an intervention. I recently overheard a parent venting to a friend—another parent in the school—about a child's homework load. The friend said, "You ought to call the principal." Ideally, this option never crosses a parent's mind; instead, the advice they give one another should be "You should call your child's teacher." The teacher should always be the first line of communication when a conflict arises. They know the most about a child and the antecedents to a conflict. Teachers should know they are the best resolution to a conflict and accept this responsibility as part of their job.

My district recently did a large-scale survey to gather information about the community's perspective of the school district. One of the questions was about trust. An overwhelming number had faith and trust in their child's teacher. The number was significantly lower for school administrators. I didn't take this as a negative; on the contrary, it proved to me that teachers absolutely should be the point person when conflict arises. In fact, trust can grow because of conflict. Taking conflict management away from a teacher diminishes their future ability to manage it.

With that said, teachers working through conflict do benefit from the principal's support, either through coaching a teacher or through direct interventions. The following strategies can be used by either a principal or a teacher.

Act Through Communication

Of all the takeaways from this chapter, I feel most strongly about the importance of being proactive when working with parents. As I have said often in this book, there are times conflict will be resolved on its own, requiring very little direct mediation. This is much more likely to happen if appropriate communication has taken place. If a conflict arises, simply turning the parent back to the original source of information to explain structures, expectations, timelines, and outcomes can dissipate the problem. That's why parents, teachers, and principals should commit to communicating early, often, and well. My husband, an athletic director for over two decades, frequently speaks about the importance of this. Athletics is an area in which parents are known to be especially involved and reactive. Yet there are years at a time when he hears nothing from parents. Why? Because he makes sure every bit of information is communicated: schedules, programming protocols, coach expectations, playing time, and goals for each athlete's experience. Through constant reminders, he constantly funnels parents to the website for timely updates, and he expects them to reach out to coaches with any questions. He trains coaches to make communication a priority, knowing that they, too, will benefit from proactive and thorough communication. This front-end communication not only ensures information is readily available but also shows that expectations and processes have been implemented with consistency. And why is that important? Because it builds trust.

As a principal, I often worked with staff to effectively communicate with parents, reminding them that when parents trust the professionalism and skill of a teacher, coach, paraprofessional, office staff, or intervention specialist, they are far less likely to want the principal to intervene. As mentioned earlier, pushback is usually the result of a parent not understanding why something happened or questioning the reasoning behind it. Teachers avoid this if they communicate smart, communicate clearly, and communicate often.

- **Communicate smart:** Communicating with parents does not have to take a lot of time and effort. A website, a private social media group, emails, and newsletter templates are all tools that can make communication quick and easy, especially with practice and routine. Finding the best communication mode for a community of parents saves hours in lost efforts.

- **Communicate clearly:** Parents don't have a lot of time to read. Communication should be clear, concise, and factual. Bullet points and summaries are invaluable to parents.

- **Communicate often:** My rule of thumb has always been this: If I think I'm communicating enough, I am probably halfway there. Creating a consistent rhythm of regular communication will train parents to know when and how information will be provided.

Also noteworthy is the importance of constantly reflecting on how we communicate. I once worked with a teacher who tried to be proactive in communication but was dismayed that his efforts fell flat. "I send out a newsletter every week, but parents don't read it, and then they are mad when they don't know what is happening." I asked him to show me a few samples. I immediately recognized the problem. His mistake was repeating the same information. Yes, he sent a weekly newsletter—a great idea—but he repeated information over and over again for weeks at a time. If a project was coming up, he'd put it in the newsletter two months ahead of time and then copy and paste the same paragraph for eight weeks running. Any new information got lost in the old information. Parents had indeed stopped reading it because they were likely assuming it was all repeat information. My suggestion is to put the information in the newsletter once and then compile repeat information on a website or easily accessible link. Even the words "see previous news-letters here," linked to an archive, can help train parents about where to find information.

Another common barrier to communication is when staff assume parents already know things. I see this with veteran teachers or athletic coaches. They are so used to their schedules and systems they forget that the fresh batch of students or athletes is starting with zero information. Approaching all communication as if the parent is a beginner is a great strategy—it guarantees information will be thorough and helpful.

Act Through Outreach

So many schools have excellent outreach programs to get parents into the school and to be part of the community. Open houses, academic meetings, game night, awards celebrations, PTO, and volunteer pro-grams are all ways that parents can feel part of their child's school expe-rience. Many high schools host events for theater, music, or athletics, in which they specifically invite younger students and their families—an excellent way to start early building trust and marketing their programs to the larger community. Parents who know their presence is genuinely appreciated and welcomed will give the teachers and principal a little grace when things get difficult.

Act Through Listening

Poor listening practices escalate conflict. Close listening deescalates it. Especially when angry or upset, parents deserve to be heard, even when their words do not match what they are trying to say. This is a concept we discuss in several other places in this book, but as an example, think of a parent who says, "Are you implying my child isn't telling you the truth? My child would *never* lie." Close listening might tell us the parent is actu-ally trying to communicate, "I do not want to believe my child would lie." In another example, if they say, "I'm not the only parent who feels this way," they may be trying to communicate that they feel so frustrated that they have reached out to friends to create a sense of comradeship and solidarity so that they don't feel so alone. Careful listening gets to the root of the real problem—a necessity in resolving conflicts.

Act Through Acceptance

Rather than be defensive or deny a parent's perspective, we should accept and even embrace it. Even if we think it's misguided or misinformed, what they think and how they feel is real. A rebuke or denial of their point of view will just intensify their desire to be understood and believed. It's far better to have the mindset that a parent's perspective is legitimate and valuable—right from the start.

Even in cases where a parent brings unreasonable or irrational views, we can't simply tell them they are wrong. We have to accept their viewpoint, recognize we will not change it, and respond accordingly. Principals felt this acutely during the COVID crisis, in which schools were held to specific health requirements and some parents refused to comply. I found success by acknowledging their views—"I understand your stance and recognize your commitment to it"—but then followed with "In the school setting, though, we need to adjust your expectations for the safety and well-being of others." I didn't get into who was right or wrong; I simply stuck to facts, policy, and mandates. This applies, too, if a parent brings hateful or discriminatory views to a school setting. A parent once set up a meeting with me and insisted a teacher be disciplined for having photographs of his husband on his desk. I explained that the Supreme Court has ruled on this issue, so it is no longer a topic for discussion. The teacher has a right to display a photograph of his family. I did not attempt to change the parent's mind but also did not engage in an argument with him.

Act Through Honesty and Reassurance

When communicating with parents, we can be truthful about the challenges we're facing *and* be reassuring, all at the same time. This happens through a solutions-based approach. "As I explain the challenges I'm facing, I'll also share my plan for improvement." Parents find reassurance when they work with teachers who identify problems and know how to solve them.

Act with Focus on Students

Rather than discuss other children, teachers should keep all conversation and solutions about that parent's child. Sometimes there are social repercussions involving other students, but our focus should be on *this problem, this child, this parent, and this solution.*

Act with Long-Term Goals

Rather than hoping for a quick fix, we should consider long-term outcomes. Educating students isn't about the moment—it's about thousands of moments, culminating in a long learning journey. Considering the long-term effects of decisions shouldn't be done just to avoid conflict but also because it's the best opportunity to know what matters and what doesn't. Especially in situations of conflict, offering parents the long view can be surprisingly reassuring and can deescalate the anxiety of a single moment or situation.

Act by Taking Responsibility

It must be frustrating to be a parent, to know there was a staff misstep, and to hear deflection of blame. It's far better for staff to say, "Wow, I wish I hadn't done it that way. I made a mistake. This is what I've learned and how I can make it right."

Act with Evolution

I admire principals and school staff who are always looking to evolve their communication practices. To expand on an earlier example, if a teacher is sending a parent newsletter home in backpacks every week and no one reads it, they should abandon that practice and communicate in a way that will work. Maybe it's on a social media or communication app; maybe it's by having the students create a messaging system through email or a learning management system; maybe it's by short videos posted on a private website. Experimenting on ways to get the right information out and make sure it is received will pay huge dividends.

Managing Escalating Conflict

Now that we've discussed ways to avoid conflict before it happens—through communication and building trust—let's think about what to do if there is a conflict for which a principal must intervene. This happens when a teacher feels unable, unequipped, or not confident to resolve it on their own, often after emotion has overtaken the original issue. Here are a few considerations to get started.

Know When to Step in

I try to stay out of teacher–parent conflicts unless I know they are at a stalemate or nothing will improve until I get involved. Sometimes a teacher asks for help, but more often, an intervention request comes from a parent who feels they are out of options and wants to speak to the principal to get solid answers "from the top." In each case, I always ask if the two have spoken together. If not, I will encourage them to do so; if they refuse or seem unable, I'll agree to get involved. There is no sure-fire set of steps to guarantee success, because the response will vary with the situation and details. There are times I have sat down with both parties and helped mediate toward a solution. More often I have determined, through preemptive conversations, that it's best to meet with each party alone. I make this decision after thoroughly researching the situation and thinking through my intended outcome.

Ask and Learn

When conflict between parents and a staff member escalates, I study the situation. I ask to review any previous communication if possible—emails, voicemails, and messages sent through a school-approved app or learning management system. I ask the teacher for a summary of what happened. I patch together the parents' perspective from their communication with me or what students or staff members have said. I will try to have a thorough understanding of the facts leading to the conflict so that I feel I'm part of it and understand all the details.

Set the Table

Deciding how your involvement will look is an important step. As an example, you may want to resolve the situation with a phone call, or you may want an in-person meeting. You'll want to decide who should be in the conversation, what the goals or outcomes should be, and what potential solutions you have available. You may have the conflicting parties come together; you may meet with them individually. It all depends on how you think you can reach your desired outcome.

Don't Let It Become a Bash Session

If the mediation happens individually, you'll want to keep the conversation professional. The parent cannot be permitted to slander a teacher, nor can a teacher outline all the things a parent has done wrong. There is a clear line between allowing someone space to vent their frustrations and letting it turn personal and ugly. Although it's sometimes difficult to find that line, I usually know it's been crossed if I find myself feeling uncomfortably defensive of the other person. In those cases, I give a simple reminder: "Let's try to avoid letting this negative experience turn personal" or "In keeping this professional, let's focus again on what happened and how we can resolve it."

Don't Defend Bad Behavior

If a teacher has acted inappropriately or unprofessionally, it's perfectly OK to say as much to the parent, although word choice is important here—again, you don't want to say anything negative about the teacher's skills or intentions. Instead, you might say, "The decisions made in this case do not reflect our school's typical practices," or, "I apologize for this error in judgment. I hope you will allow us grace as we work to ensure we never replicate this situation again."

Make a Plan and Follow Up

As part of resolving the conflict, you will want to make a clear plan and share it with everyone involved. This is part of the *act* step of conflict resolution. You'll want to decide what changes will be implemented, who is responsible for those changes, and how you will follow up. You will have little control over how a parent will react once the situation is resolved, but you do have influence on the teacher's response. They tend to lose confidence if confronted by a parent, so they may need reassurance that you believe in them. They will also appreciate your honest feedback. Your follow-up can include a summarization of your takeaways from the situation and what you hope will change as a result of it.

The 1 Percent

These strategies and solutions work for most parents, but every now and then, we encounter a parent who seems intent on refusing all compromise and solutions. As stated earlier, it's a very small percentage—perhaps less than 1 percent—but this small percentage can pack a punch. These are the parents who seem to seek conflict and enjoy the escalation of it. At best, these parents can make us question our effectiveness; at worst, they can bully us, defame us, and make us fear for our jobs.

My second year as an assistant principal, one of our parents almost drove me to leave education altogether. Her children had many needs, and no matter what we did to support them, she fought against us and said terrible things about us to her children. She sent five or six emails a day to the teachers and me, demanding a response and not relenting until she got one; when we finally replied, she would decimate every word in the response. We would defend ourselves, and then the cycle would begin again. Round and round it went. Over time, I accumulated thousands of pages of emails from her. Attempting a fix, I encouraged staff to avoid emailing her, but phone calls proved to be worse; she would interpret our words in ways that made us seem wicked and incompetent and then quote us—out of context—in another series of emails she sent to our Board of Education.

We tried to focus only on what we could control, educating her children and staying clinical in our approach, but it was impossible to do, especially when the children, encouraged by their mother, began misquoting teachers, reporting things that had not occurred, and misrepresenting conversations. The children developed troubling behaviors, including being rude to teachers and cruel to their peers. Teachers were afraid to implement plans or consequences, knowing the parent would rage against any attempts the teachers made, so they often sent the children to me in the principal's office. I became the parent's primary target. She threatened to sue me personally, threatened to go to the superintendent, the board, and local media, and even filed a complaint with our state education office to have me stripped of my license.

To this day, when I think of this parent, I have a physical, anxious reaction. I suffered mostly alone, feeling I had to accept this treatment in order to protect the teachers. It was a horrible experience. It only ended when the children went to their next school, at which point the parent's venom was pointed at my high school colleague.

It took me a long time and a lot of reflection to accept the experience as one that made me stronger and improved my leadership skills. I've since helped colleagues in similar situations, and I will be ready if I find myself at the receiving end of another abusive parent. I'll use the following strategies to remain strong and stable as I manage the impact on teachers and our school.

Document

Keep a log of every interaction you have with the parent. Although I generally encourage phone calls, email might be a better tool in cases like this, because it decreases the risk of conversations being misrepresented or misquoted later. It also creates a full picture of your attempts at making peace.

Set Communication Guardrails

I recently worked with a principal who was receiving multiple emails a day, much like I described above. I encouraged him to inform the parent that unless her child's safety was a concern, he would reply to her only twice a week—Tuesdays and Fridays—to provide answers to her questions. Then I told him to only respond to legitimate questions. "Don't take the bait," I said, referring to the parent's tendency to frame teachers through passive accusations. "Only sentences that end with a question mark should get a response." I also encouraged short, factual, concise responses. "Don't over-explain. If the question can be answered with a yes or no, that's all you need to use."

Record

I am generally against recording conversations with parents, as it creates an environment of mistrust and prohibits genuine connection. However, with parents who are likely to misrepresent your conversation, you may consider asking the parent if the conversations can be recorded. I only do this if the parent has previously misrepresented things I have said or if I know or suspect the parent is also recording. In some states, such as mine, the parent does not need consent to record a conversation, and nor do I. I am, however, committed to transparency. I always tell a parent if I am recording, even knowing they do not need to offer the same respect to me. Having a record of a conversation protects me from being quoted out of context.

Consult with an Attorney

Although legal support is expensive, most districts have an attorney on retainer. A friend of mine, who serves as a superintendent on the East Coast, stepped in after teachers and principals were so mistreated by a parent that there were genuine concerns about their mental health. He hired an attorney to be the liaison, forbidding anyone on his staff to respond to the parent. The attorney answered all emails and managed all communication. Meetings were held virtually. Everyone was on mute until asked to speak by the attorney, who decided who was able to speak and when. It was expensive, because the attorney spent many billable hours as an intermediary between the school and parent, but it was worth every penny to protect the mental and professional health of the teachers and principal.

Don't Be Gaslighted

The worst thing about a parent this aggressive is that you might begin to question yourself and your own sanity. It's important not to let this happen. Stay connected to what you know to be true. Find a colleague who can reassure you that you're not losing your mind. The strength is in you; hang on to it as tightly as you can.

Ask for Help

A principal reached out to me last year, having begun to have panic attacks just thinking of one particular parent in his building. I suggested he see a doctor to rule out any health issues, but I also encouraged him to reach out to his supervisor to discuss the situation. Suffering alone is the worst kind of suffering. Having someone understand the pain and loneliness of attacks helps absorb some of the inner difficulty that accompanies it. It can also open up potential solutions from someone who isn't so emotionally exhausted by the cycle of abuse.

Fortunately, parents with this intensity do not represent the vast majority of parents. Most conflicts are manageable, especially by following an anticipate-analyze-act process. Parents are generally extremely supportive of their children's teacher, and with strong proactive communication, relationships with them will be built on a strong foundation of trust.

It also helps to have a staff with a strong, healthy mindset about working with parents. I thought of this recently when I ran into one of my favorite people—a 3rd grade teacher in a school I once led. We don't work together anymore, but I'd always admired and respected her relationships with parents. Skilled and experienced, she often had the most challenging students in her classroom. When I saw her, I was thinking about writing this book, so I took the opportunity to ask how she always managed to avoid conflict with parents, especially given some of the complex home-to-school situations that had come her way. She smiled. "It's simple," she said. "Every time I get frustrated with a child, I think, 'You are someone's baby.' And every time I get frustrated with a parent,

I think, 'You are someone's parent.' The child is someone's whole entire world. I'm just the teacher, and this is just one year in a long life. I give all I can give, and that has to be enough."

She is right. Empathy helps keep conflict in perspective, and a rational mindset keeps it from diminishing a teacher's confidence and effectiveness. Conflict won't always be resolved completely; there are times it can just be managed, and accepting this truth is part of leadership. Remember—some conflict is healthy, as it helps us improve and be better at what we do. In the end, a relationship with parents, even through conflict, comes down to doing the best we can do—and letting that be enough.

8

When the Conflict Is You

There are times in every principal's career in which everything seems like a mess. There is conflict, disorganization, and low morale. No one seems happy. Stress is high. During these times, it's natural to pause and wonder, *Am I doing* anything *right?* Bad days happen, and when they do, the weight of all those missteps feels heavy, as if the principal is alone against the rest of the world.

There is a popular Facebook group with over 50,000 principals as members. Occasionally a principal will post about feeling inadequate, overwhelmed, and overcome by conflict. They explain how they are mistreated by their staff, not respected by students, or have fractured relationships with parents. They ask for insight and advice to move forward. Comments from other group members quickly validate the principal, offering advice to overcome the negative opinions. They encourage the principal to stay strong, push through, and maintain a positive mindset.

Like those commenters, I naturally jump to the defense of principals. I feel such empathy that they go to work every day and feel devalued and mistreated. No one should spend their days in that kind of environment. Indeed, some schools have a toxic culture in which it is simply impossible to please anyone, no matter what one does. In that spirit, it's important to acknowledge, early in this chapter, there are some environments so negative and destructive that the principal risks their own mental or physical health if they stay. Sometimes leaving is the only solution.

I have consulted with several principals who have had to make the difficult decision to leave a noxious school and find a position elsewhere. I have counseled them through this with the reminder that health and professional satisfaction must be a priority. One of my favorite phrases is "Go where you're wanted."

In direct contradiction, another of my favorite phrases is "Bloom where you're planted." While some toxic situations are unfixable, it is also true that in some toxic situations, a skilled leader can, with time and perseverance, improve a negative school culture. It takes a deep inner strength to dig in and overcome a difficult environment and even more strength to look inside and ask hard questions about the role of one's own leadership.

A friend of mine recently told me about doing this type of internal audit. "Everything was a disaster," he said. There was constant conflict in his building, and most of the school community blamed him for it. "Teachers didn't like me, students hated me, and parents fought me on everything." He began to wonder, *What if the problem is me? What if it is my leadership that is flaming this fire?*

I respected him for asking these questions and for taking the time to look inward. It took courage to consider if his actions were actually increasing—rather than reducing—incidents of conflict. His high-level reflection and soul searching allowed him to evaluate the connection between his leadership and the problems plaguing his school.

How, though? First, principals can audit their leadership by seeking feedback from internal stakeholders. Many principals survey their staff, either formally or informally, to identify patterns and make leadership changes. Second, feedback from students and parents should be considered because their insight can provide an additional view of a leader's impact. A third strategy is to seek input from trusted colleagues and mentors. In my first years as a principal, I was lucky enough to have an honest, straightforward superintendent who kindly and consistently told me where I needed to improve. He truly wanted to help me become a strong leader, and I trusted him implicitly. His feedback helped me see some of the mistakes I was making. He taught me to be the kind of leader who manages conflict rather than exacerbates it. Other colleagues and friends, such as assistant principals and administrative assistants with whom I've worked over the years, have also given me invaluable feedback on my leadership. Along the way, I have been able to identify common missteps leaders might make that could create a culture of conflict. Let's look at a few of them, and let's do it with an eye on the anticipate-analyze-act process. Identifying yourself in these missteps will help you anticipate problems and, ideally, avoid them altogether.

Anticipate Common Missteps

Avoiding Responsibility

Principals who are quick to point fingers away from themselves when things go wrong create an environment of blame deflection. The instinct to assign fault to others is natural and might often be spot-on, but in doing so, the principal will develop a reputation of finding excuses rather than solutions. I have been in many situations when I didn't feel responsible for something going wrong but, upon reflection, recognized that I did own part (or all) of the problem. As an example, I once signed a required district form giving permission for a team to take an out-of-state trip. I was the fourth and final person required to sign it. Not long afterward, it was determined by the transportation department that the trip should never have been approved. I badly wanted to blame the three people who had preceded me—shouldn't they have known to deny the trip before it even got to my desk? No. I owned the problem just as much as they did—perhaps more so because I was responsible for making sure the previous three signees knew the rules about trips. As much as I wanted to blame them, I couldn't. The mistake was my fault.

Defensiveness

For some reason, many people like to "catch" a principal in a mistake. A few that come to mind are staff members who ask questions in staff meetings with an accusatory tone, parents who quote obscure policy and law in efforts to overturn a decision, or students who accuse principals of tones or words they did not use. It's easy to feel inflamed by these conversations and react in a defensive, angry, or aggressive manner. This is a common misstep but important to avoid, as defensiveness can unintentionally imply wrongdoing.

Lack of Trust

If you feel like no one trusts you, it might be true. As difficult as it is, you might want to ask yourself why. Principals who do not follow through on promises, do not tackle difficult problems, or do not successfully prioritize may find themselves leading a staff that doesn't have faith in their leadership or trust the things they say.

Questionable Honesty

Similarly, it's a bad idea for principals to communicate unverified or incorrect information, fudge the truth, or deliberately present information inaccurately. A principal might do this with good intentions, especially when trying to soften bad news. They may also do it when it just seems easier than the difficult truth. It is likely to backfire, though, into developing a reputation of being dishonest.

Compromised Integrity

It is often said that doing the right thing when no one is watching is what defines your character. As mentioned earlier in this book, a truism for school principals is that someone is always watching. When you make choices that are not student-centered or are not aligned with your district's morals and values, it won't take long before others will begin to question your integrity.

Inconsistency

If you change your leadership style or choices based on the situation, stakeholders, or perceived outcome, your inconsistency will create frustration and conflict. Relying on policy, treating everyone fairly, and striving for equitable outcomes every time is what helps you become a leader of consistency—which helps people trust in the predictability of your decisions.

Emotional Responses

Because so much of conflict is based on feelings and personal responses, it is easy for those involved to be overcome by emotion. This is evident when working through conflict between students, especially young children who may act impulsively out of emotion. It is true with mature adults too. We are all susceptible. Principals who manage conflict based on feelings, not facts, will be seen as letting their own emotions drive their response. I am a highly emotional person, and I have learned to step away from situations in which I am unable to think clearly. I know the best gift I can give myself is time and space. The problem will still be there when I'm ready.

Analyze

Now that we have anticipated how avoiding common missteps might improve our leadership, let's move into the next part of the three-step conflict resolution process.

If staff, students, or the community holds negative perceptions of your leadership, it might be that your leadership needs some improvement. Let's analyze some strategies and options you might use to counter these missteps and strengthen your reputation as a strong leader.

Take Responsibility and Avoid Blame

Early in my career, when I was eager to appear experienced, wise, and all-knowing, I would instinctively look to blame others when things went wrong. Regardless of whether I had a role in the problem or not, I would try to identify who was responsible for it. I regret this approach, because I have learned it is just as easy to say, "As the principal, I should have had a better handle on this whole situation." I've also said, "Wow, I missed a few important opportunities along the way. I wish I had done some things differently, and I'll make sure we improve the next time this situation pops up." Combining the *I* with others involved—*we*—takes some of the isolation out of accepting responsibility.

Principals who model this approach will create space for teachers to do the same. A few years ago, I was visiting a school and heard a teacher talking to a student who'd had a meltdown during a class transition. It started when the student, who was on the autism spectrum, had grown furious when asked to put away her work before she was done with it. She'd upended her chair and thrown her supplies against the wall then began sobbing uncontrollably. I passed by the teacher and student as they sat in the hall, processing the incident. "I know you were frustrated, and part of it is my fault for not recognizing you needed more time to finish your work. I am so sorry for the role I played in this." Notably, she didn't follow with a *but*. As explained in Chapters 2 and 5, this is a wise strategy for almost any situation. She simply apologized and waited for the student to say the next thing. Guess what the student said? "Sorry. You gave me warnings. I just didn't want to listen." Together, the two were able to share responsibility and begin planning for ways to avoid repeating the whole scenario. When the student returned to class, I asked the teacher about the conversation. She said, "I see my principal take responsibility all the time, and he values it in teachers and students too. In this school, knowing our principal will own his actions shows teachers and students we should do the same."

Principals don't always need to take full blame, especially when they truly have no role in the problem; in fact, doing so can be seen as placating or covering up real issues. Instead, the principal can refuse to assign blame to anyone. They can explicitly say, "Let's not point fingers at others. It's unfortunate it happened, but let's look at solutions so we can move on and not replicate this scenario again." Indeed, in many situations, there really is no one to blame, or there might be so many people involved that everyone owns a small part of it. Events occur all the time—a minor misunderstanding, an accident, an unintended or unfortunate outcome—and it's perfectly OK to say, "We were all acting with the best of intentions. No one is at fault, so let's all agree to look forward rather than backward."

Open Receptiveness

I believe it is possible to train ourselves to embrace information and feedback without being defensive. Even if the sender's tone seems to be one that accuses or blames you, forcing yourself to receive, understand, and accept the other person's point of view can soften a charged conversation. You don't have to agree—you just need to listen and hear. I have a colleague who has mastered this skill. When questioned or pushed in uncomfortable ways, she will reply with responses like "Yes, I understand," "OK," and "I hear you" in a tone that is honest, open, and kind. Using this approach, it never takes long until the contentiousness turns into a productive conversation.

Build Trust

When trust has been broken or eroded, principals should put consistent and intentional focus on strengthening it. I find that an accountability partner can be very helpful in these situations. An assistant, a mentor, a secretary, or a guidance counselor might be able to help you see when your decisions are risking the trust you've built. If you aren't ready for a colleague to be your accountability partner, you might consider reaching out to talk to a professional coach, who might be able to quickly identify ways your actions are killing trust. As an example, I once coached a principal who seemed to enjoy trying to catch teachers making mistakes. He would pull a student from a fire drill to see if teachers were taking accurate attendance; he would monitor lesson plans to see if the teachers adhered to planning; he would go into teachers' digital gradebooks to monitor the time stamp on when they entered grades. He truly believed these actions would help teachers improve.

When I told him his actions were destroying trust, he was shocked. I told him, "When teachers know their principal is trying to catch them in a mistake, they think you are working against them. It will take a long time to get them to trust you again." I urged him to immediately stop being a "gotcha" principal and instead be a "withya" principal—in other words, he should align with the teachers to maximize their strengths rather than find out their failures. Within just a few coaching sessions, the principal had a better idea of how to build trust with his school community.

Be Honest

There are two ways to share information with staff, students, and parents: openly and honestly, or by saying you *can't* be open and honest—and explaining why. The approach that won't work? Saying things that aren't true. I know of a principal who lost her job for this. She struggled to share even the simplest of information in an honest and accurate way. Once staff and parents recognized her words didn't match outcomes or actions, she developed a reputation as a liar. In my heart, I don't think she actually intended to lie. Instead, she changed the truth in the moment, anxious to protect herself and her staff; she hated making people mad or upsetting them, so she would leave out truthful details in order to soften bad news. Worse, she had a tendency to embellish information to enhance her role in particular situations. When there were conflicts with students and the parents resisted the outcomes, she would make promises that were impossible to keep; when called on it, she would make up yet another untruth and make yet another impossible promise. The dishonestly piled up.

Being honest is nonnegotiable for a principal. Students, staff, and community need to know the things they hear their principal say are true. With this foundation of honesty, a school community will not look at the principal negatively when information changes, especially if they know the "why" behind change. If they feel information is consistently false, they will be unable to forgive.

Being honest doesn't mean sharing all the information all the time. In fact, leaving information out in order to protect others or follow the law is a form of honesty, especially when it is explained as such. Here are some phrases that might work:

- It is my goal to be honest with you, but I'm only sharing what I know is true. I'm leaving out any information that is not yet verified, and I have no way of predicting if additional information will arise later.
- I know you'd like more information, but I cannot share the details you'd like because they are not yet clear and a plan is not in place.
- Rather than give you information that isn't true, I am not sharing all the details.
- As soon as I can share information, I will.

- Honestly, it is important to me, and I know it is important for you.
- I am unable to share specific details, but please don't mistake omission as me hiding something. I'm telling you everything I am able to share.

As with anything, these phrases are much better received if they are said with a kind, authentic tone—not one that highlights a power differential or makes the other person feel small.

Act with Integrity

Principals process hundreds of decisions each day, both small and large. Most of these decisions are made quickly and without much thought, but bigger decisions require pausing to sift through relevant factors and then outlining a course of action. In both cases, the goal should be to make decisions that put students first, are ethical and appropriate, follow district policy and guidelines, and provide for a positive learning environment for all stakeholders. I imagine a three-legged stool with three components holding equal weight—student safety and experience, legal mandates, and financial responsibility (see Figure 8.1). If I act without considering all of these factors, the entire stool collapses—and so does my leadership integrity.

Figure 8.1 Three-Legged Stool

Consistency

As you mediate and manage conflict, you'll want people to know you can be counted on to respond with calm intentionality. This can be done by frequently revisiting the guidelines, policies, and standards for which you are responsible, comparing your response to similar situations you have mediated, and landing on a positive outcome. Stakeholders will know that regardless of the situation, they will be heard, their perspectives will be valued, and conflict will be resolved in the best possible way.

Respond without Emotion

I mentioned earlier that I am an emotional person. Although I am not always successful, I work very hard to regulate my emotions when making leadership decisions. About 10 years ago, I failed thoroughly in this effort. It was one day before school started after the winter break. Several teachers had come in over the break to hang special student projects in the hallways outside their rooms. A surprise walkthrough by the fire marshal did not go well. He was new to his job, and this was his very first school inspection. He was eager to get everything right. He informed me—coldly and firmly—that all the student projects and classroom decorations had to come down. The walls needed to be empty to ensure fire prevention protocol was met. I was speechless. In years of fire inspections, I'd never needed to tell teachers to avoid hanging student projects. I tried to explain that schools are places in which student work should be displayed, that the culture of creativity and collaboration starts with the visuality of the items on the walls. Our fire safety protocols were all in place, I said: all our furniture had been treated with fire retardant, our sprinkler system was up-to-date, alarms had been tested, we adhered to a drill schedule, and, by the way, I pointed out, it had been six decades since a fire in one of our nation's schools led to a student death. He stared at me stoically and said, "Do you want your school to be the first one in six decades to have a student death?"

I sputtered. "Of course not!"

"Then everything must come down. Today."

Just the thought of removing all the beautiful student work—and of telling the teachers their efforts would not be able to be celebrated—made me furious. My voice rose, and I felt my hands shaking. Just in time, I recognized I needed to get away from the situation before my emotions took over. I went outside and began walking, at first just breathing hard, and eventually working to calm my mind. After about 30 minutes, I turned around to head back to school, reminding myself with every step that the fire marshal was just doing his job and that job—keeping people safe—was not unlike my job. *There must be a compromise somewhere,* I thought. That is when I knew I'd regulated my emotions.

Back at school, the fire marshal had left, but there was a message given to my secretary that he was coming back—this time with his chief. I assumed they were going to come at me two against one, so I took another walk, this time through the school's halls, and prepared a calm, reasonable response. Some items on the walls probably should be taken down, I realized, as they were old and outdated. When the chief and marshal arrived, I met them, apologized, and asked if we could find some middle ground. Indeed, the chief said, he was happy to allow student work to be displayed, provided no more than a certain percentage of walls were covered. The new marshal was following protocol, he said, but we could come to a reasonable compromise so the students could still have their work highlighted. In the end, it was a good outcome, as I encouraged teachers to remove months-old work and only keep what mattered most to their students at that time.

The situation would not have ended well had I let my emotions say all the things I wanted to say. It takes discipline and skill to manage emotion, especially when instinct tells you to defend or protect the work, time, and efforts of your students and staff. Excusing yourself to get a better handle on your thoughts is a sign of strong leadership and will communicate to others that you will not be provoked or pushed into a response clouded by emotion.

With thoughtful analysis of your responses to conflict situation, we've moved toward completing the circle of anticipate-analyze-act. We will finish by considering actions you can take to improve your effectiveness in working through conflict.

Act

To be a strong leader, we can rely on certain approaches to be our best. Often, the most important action is to practice patience, empathy, and compassion whenever possible. When people are in conflict with one another, it's a good bet they are feeling anxious and upset. They'll need someone to hear their perspective and acknowledge an understanding of the intensity and root of their feelings. Let's think of a few other actionable strategies to use.

Maximize Your Style

As with any other situation in working through conflict, principals tend to have a wide spectrum of styles. Let's look at this through the lens of student behaviors. Some principals approach investigations softly and gently. I know an assistant principal whose mantra is "All behavior is communication, and every communication adds value." In working through conflict, her goal is to use forgiving, supportive language to get to the root of what negative feeling is being communicated. In the same building, another assistant principal rejects this softer style, instead taking a tough, no-nonsense approach. He relies exclusively on the district's code of conduct by identifying behavior and deciding on a consequence. As with anything, finding somewhere in the middle is probably the most effective—to approach each student with kindness while also following policy and sticking to appropriate consequences.

Consider Criticism

Not long ago, I spoke with a principal who was often criticized by her staff for not drawing a hard line when students argued or fought with one another. Teachers thought her only intervention was to listen to the students, be sympathetic, ask them to stop engaging in disruptive behavior, give them both a treat, and send them back to class. "Go to the office, leave with a cookie and a diploma," a teacher once snapped at her. But the principal felt this criticism was unfair. In one incident, a student had been bullying another student for quite some time, and many other students had taken sides and were having great fun egging it on. There were rumors of an after-school physical altercation. Together with the school's guidance counselor, the principal called both students down to the office to help them work out the problem. It was a difficult afternoon, with both students very upset and rehashing weeks of arguments and disagreements, mostly done on social media. A truce seemed elusive, but the principal and counselor were able to guide both students to acknowledge their roles and admit they wanted to move forward. Finally, after several hours, both students agreed to avoid one another and stop discussing the fight. In a phone call, both parents explained how they would hold their children accountable at home. With the issue seemingly solved, the principal allowed both students to take a mint from her candy bowl and go back to class.

Indeed, it did not look good. Both students returned to class, smiling and eating candy, with no disciplinary action following them. Worse yet, it wasn't the quick fix the principal had hoped for; with so many other students involved, the rumors and disruption continued throughout the day. To teachers, it appeared as if the mediation had failed. In fact, several teachers complained to the guidance counselor that the principal's "bleeding heart" was making her ineffective. In short, the teachers wanted the students suspended, but the principal did not believe in suspension as an effective disciplinary tool. The principal was dismayed at the division in beliefs. "I did the right thing! I helped the students work through their issues and gave them the opportunity to try again! Why are they so critical of what I'm trying to do?"

I told her I didn't think she was wrong, but I thought she should consider the consistent criticism she received. If *everyone* thinks you're too soft, maybe you are. If *everyone* feels uninformed, perhaps you're not being informative. I suggested she could take a more proactive approach by giving teachers a voice in specifying their criticism. If it was the candy that bothered them, she could stop giving candy when students returned to class. If it was suspension they wanted, she could develop a subcommittee to discuss the negative repercussions for suspension and brainstorm other potential options. If they were being critical because they didn't know enough details about the outcomes, she could set up after-school office hours to explain the complicated nuances behind behavior decisions. Incorporating the perspectives of teachers would help her feel less alone in trying to do the right thing. The current situation was damaging her credibility and confidence, so it was time for her to identify frequent criticisms and develop a plan to address them.

Ask for Outside Perspective

As with the example above, it is common for principals to feel very alone when helping others work through conflict, especially because critical eyes evaluate everything we do. Of course, these critical eyes often have incomplete information; they might not be in the room during a conflict intervention, and those who *are* in the room do not always share complete, unbiased facts. It can feel terribly isolating.

To overcome this, I try to gather an outside perspective to give me a clear view of the situation. Many online principal groups offer a platform to do this. Posters can provide background information for other group members—teachers and principals—to weigh in. Many good ideas and insights can come from these anonymous responses. Although there are limitations—a "blind perspective" doesn't capture the nuances of personality and history of a specific situation—sometimes that is exactly what is needed. Something that seems acceptable to internal stakeholders might seem outrageous to someone not embroiled in it. This happened not long ago with a principal I know. She had a problematic staff member, Ms. B, who never communicated with parents. It had been Ms. B's approach for so long that no one questioned it. When one of her students tantrumed during a school assembly, the principal asked Ms. B to call the parent and explain what happened. Ms. B refused. "I won't," she said. "That call should come from you."

The principal was taken aback. Could a teacher refuse to contact a parent about a child in that teacher's class? First, the principal asked for perspective from the previous principal, now working at the district office. He rolled his eyes and said, "Yep, that sounds about right. Ms. B doesn't talk to parents about behaviors. I always had to do it. You might as well just pick up the phone and get it over with." Although the current principal was bothered by this approach, it did indeed seem like something so ingrained in the school's culture it was never going to change. To check on her own incredulity, she told the story to a colleague who knew nothing of Ms. B. The colleague said, "No. A teacher cannot refuse to call a parent about a behavior in class." This was a simple, clear, unbiased perspective, and it was exactly what the principal needed. She went back to Ms. B and explained the expectation that the parent needed to be called. To help, she offered to be in the room when the call was made. Ms. B was not happy, but she did it. After that, the principal continued to ask Ms. B to be the first line of communication with her students' behaviors. The rest of the staff was quietly pleased that Ms. B was finally held to the same expectation they'd been held to for so long. In this case, had the principal agreed to make all the behavior calls, she would have enabled Ms. B to continue her disengagement with parents— and would have set an unfair precedent for future conflicts.

Look for Your Own Bias

We all have biases. It is impossible to be human and not feel our- selves pulled to a particular perspective or side of an argument. This is especially true when we have to continuously intervene with the same student, teacher, or parent. I once worked with a parent who was so high maintenance, so aggressive, and so easily offended I grew to dread the sight of her number lighting up my office phone. She created problems where there should be none. She would interrogate her child every after- noon when he got off the bus, looking for little nuggets of information she could turn into a problem. She called me almost daily to criticize teachers, students, or our school in general. Her attacks often turned personal, too, with implications that I was a weak or ignorant leader.

Whenever I spoke with her, even without knowing what issue she might bring forward, I'd already decided she was wrong. It was a bias that made me defensive and resentful. To work around this bias, I decided I needed to put up some guardrails. I mobilized a team approach—the teacher, counselor, and I took turns replying to her calls and emails, and we only responded if she had a specific question we could answer. Before responding, we would meet briefly to unify our thinking and stay aligned. In addition to alleviating the pressure on the three of us to individually respond to the parent's relentless questions, having a team approach helped tamp down my own bias and keep me at my professional best.

Get to the Root of Misunderstandings

When conflict is ongoing and your stakeholders consider you responsible, you will likely feel misunderstood and unfairly blamed. In these situations, it's worth taking some time to dig into why the misunderstanding occurred and where it originated. Are others trying to communicate with you but you are not hearing them? Or are they not hearing what you are trying to communicate? Effective communication, both as a speaker and as a listener, is a powerful antithesis to these problems. We should speak with intention and check for understanding—just as we expect teachers to do with their students. As you sift through the layers that come with close listening, you can ask follow-up questions such as "I want to be certain I'm hearing and understanding. Is it OK if I say this back to you?" Diligence in communication provides clarity for everyone involved.

Look for Trends

If you are always mired in some sort of conflict, you might think about how you can change your approach. Unfortunately, the principal's job is not one where a clear path is always evident. A principal contacted me recently and told me he felt he was living in a school-based Goldilocks reenactment. "Some teachers think I'm too tough. Some think I'm too soft. Some think I respond to parents too quickly. Others think it takes me too long. Some wish I got more involved in team discussions and disagreements; others wish I would stay out of it. Some say I'm too empathetic; others say I am cold-hearted. I can't win!" I related deeply to this principal's frustration, especially when he asked, "Do you have any ideas of what I might do differently?"

It was a good question. I encouraged him to look inside himself and identify patterns. When does conflict emerge the most? Is it only between students? Are the students in a place of relative peace, but the staff can't seem to get along? Maybe it is a consistent discord among parents or the community. Perhaps conflict arises after a specific event—a poorly planned staff meeting, a pep rally, a dance, or an assembly. Identifying trends might illuminate a larger problem, such as poor communication, lack of follow-through, outdated processes, or a leadership structure that is failing. It might be because expectations are not clear, cliques are permitted, or resources are inequitable. Again, these are not easy questions to answer, but an honest self-audit might reveal some hard truths that lead to positive change.

Accept Some Stalemates

There is simply no way to please everyone. Last year, I mentored a new principal who was eager to be a strong liaison between her school and the small rural community in which she worked. She wanted parents to see her as relatable, visible, and available. At the end of the year, she put out a survey to parents. Exactly 40 percent replied saying they found the principal to be quick to respond and easy to access. Another 40 percent said she was elusive and difficult to reach. The final 20 percent were unsure. "What am I supposed to do with this information?" she asked, flummoxed. I advised her to continue to reflect on her approach but avoid reacting to noninformation. "This data doesn't tell you anything concrete," I said. "In fact, it tells me you have a community with varying expectations." I went on to tell her what I believe to be true for all principals. You will never get 100 percent of the people to respond that you are perfect. Keep working on the 40 percent who feel you're difficult to reach, but remember that 40 percent think you're doing a great job, and 20 percent of them either don't know or don't have a strong opinion. In the end, if we keep working toward perfect results, we should know we'll never get to perfection—but it's a journey worth trying.

Unsolvable Conflict

Sometimes, there is nothing a principal can do to alleviate conflict. In one of the most challenging mediations I've ever done, two teachers intensely disliked one another. Years earlier, before I worked with either one of them, angry words had been exchanged between them; since then, there had been additional layers of frustration and discontent. I even suspected neither remembered the original issue that divided them. When I was hired as the principal, I was certain I would be able to broker some peace between the two. It bothered me that the two avoided being in a room together, and I thought I could provide opportunities for them to work together and share some success through a couple shared student initiatives. In spite of my best efforts, though, I came to realize this would never be the case. There was nothing I—or anyone else, for that matter—could do to help their years-long discontent with one another. In the end, I had to recognize their conflict was not mine to own. For a while, I felt like I had failed, but in time, I had to put it in a box and put a lid on it. It wasn't worth me losing sleep over others' refusal to make peace. It was an example of how I learned and grew as a professional myself. I am not a parent to the adults that work with me. I can try to work through problems and provide my best mediation skills. I can set expectations and ensure adherence—but I am not a miracle worker. Doing my best is the best I can do.

As we wrap up this chapter of self-reflection, it is comforting to remember that every situation of conflict brings learning. From learning we grow, improve, and find strength. When we have success, it feels good. When we fail, it feels terrible. Both have value. Although I have to work hard to remember this in myself, both success and failure offer an opportunity to do better, be better, and lead better.

9

Clarity and Confidence

By nature, educators tend to be people who like to bring others together. Conflict seems to challenge that instinct. Teachers and principals who find themselves involved in conflict might think, "I don't understand. Why can't people just get along?"

A primary takeaway of this book is that the complicated nature of human relationships, combined with the setting and complications of school, will inevitably give rise to ongoing conflict. My goal is to help principals gain confidence and clarity when managing problems between other people, using each chapter to study specific dynamics and potential ramifications of common conflicts. But, before closing, there are a few more considerations and scenarios to cover. Let's start with a common miscommunication trap many principals face.

When People Don't Say What They Mean

In many ways, communication can be both the cause and the solution to conflicts. Poor communication creates it; strong communication heals it. No principal is a perfect communicator, and we can't expect others to be perfect, either. This is especially true when we hear others say something but we know they actually mean something else. There are some phrases so commonly used by teachers and parents that they are almost expected—but can be disheartening all the same. As a principal, each time I would hear one of these things, I would feel the familiar frustration that comes from helplessness or the sense of being misunderstood. In time, though, I learned these phrases usually mean something beyond what the literal words would make me think. Here are a few examples.

What they say: "It just seems like there are no consequences anymore." This is usually said to a principal after a student behavior incident, indicating the teacher is unhappy with the outcome.

- **What they mean:** "The consequence was not big enough for the behavior." From a larger lens, they may feel the principal's approach is not stringent or that response to behavior isn't taken seriously enough.

- **How to reply:** "I'd love to know why you feel that way." Conversation is the best approach, giving the teacher a chance to explain why they feel this way. The principal can provide additional details, if appropriate, to help the teacher understand; however, as many principals can attest, it is often impossible to get universal agreement on a behavior consequence. If nothing else, listening gives a chance for the teacher to be heard.

What they say: "Just a heads-up." This is usually said to a principal by a teacher who is anxious about an incident that has recently occurred.

- **What they mean:** "There was a situation that I think I have handled, but I'm not certain it's over. If the problem comes to you, I want you to know what happened and why I responded as I did."

- **How to reply:** "I appreciate you giving me this information ahead of time. Let's review and make a plan." No one likes to be blindsided, so expressing appreciation for the information is a great start. It can also lead to a coaching session, letting the teacher know of other responses or follow-up actions to consider—not in the tone of criticism, but from someone who is collaborating by asking for guidance in finding solutions.

What they say: "But we've always done it this way." I have heard this from teachers, parents, and students who are resistant to change.

- **What they mean:** "I like the way things are right now, and I am anxious about changing things." They may need more time or explanation before they can see and process the vision being proposed.
- **How to reply:** "Can you tell me more about that?" Again, listening to the reasons for the resistance will help recognize the barriers the speaker is envisioning. Change takes time and teamwork, so together you can determine if the intended outcome is worth the potential upheaval—big, small, real, or imagined—that will come with making a change.

What they say: "Well, that's why you make the big bucks." If I won some money every time I heard this from a teacher, I *would* be making big bucks. It's usually spoken by someone who is transferring a problem to the principal, and it feels bigger than they can handle.

- **What they mean:** "I need help from someone who outranks me. Knowing you might make more money than I do helps me to not feel guilty about passing on the problem."
- **How to reply:** The best I've ever managed in response to this phrase is "I guess so." I'm always tempted to point out that per diem rates probably make my "big bucks" a losing comparison to a teacher, but this is petty and doesn't help solve the problem. I've made my professional choices, and so have they. It's far better to just nod, smile, and take a crack at the problem. "I guess so. Let me see what I can do."

What they say: "I didn't know. No one told me." This comes from a teacher, parent, or student who feels left out of some important information. Think of a teacher who misses a meeting, say, and must be called to join in after everyone else is there.

- **What they mean:** "I missed something important, I feel embarrassed about it, and I need someone to blame."

- **How to reply:** Unless it's a consistent pattern, the best response probably is "No problem. Let me get you caught up." You can re-explain the information and remind them where it was previously shared. If it is a consistent pattern, or if there are many people who are missing information, you'll want to address it differently or review your own communication strategies. Otherwise, a simple review of the missed information will solve the problem.

What they say: "Did you get my email? My text? My voicemail?" If you're someone who has a reputation for keeping up on your communication, it can become an expectation from parents and teachers, so they may say this if they haven't gotten an immediate response.

- **What they mean:** "I've sent something that feels urgent or time-sensitive to me. I haven't heard from you, which has me a little worried about when we can discuss it."
- **How to reply:** If you did read the email, you can say so and explain you haven't yet replied because you needed time to think or prepare. If possible, you might allow the discussion to happen immediately—I've often said, "Yes, I read it; let's talk about it now, and then I won't reply to the email." That saves me time later when I'm back at my computer. If you haven't read it and don't have time, you can say, "I haven't read it, but when I do, I'll reply as soon as possible." Regardless, if a response is pressing, taking care of it in the moment—with or without the information shared in the email—does, if nothing else, reduce the time you'll need to put into a reply.

What they say: "Are you busy?" This is a common question asked of principals, and it almost never is a literal question. I used to get offended. "Of *course* I am busy! I'm always busy!" Another version of this is "Got a minute?" Again, it is easy to get irritated, because rarely does someone who asks for "a minute" just need one minute. But now that I understand what they really mean, it doesn't bother me at all.

- **What they mean:** "I need you, and I hope I can get some of your time right now."
- **How to reply:** Answer the question I know they are really asking. If I can give them some time right then, I will say, "Yes, I have time for you right now!" If I truly don't have time, I give options for follow-up. "Right now isn't a great time, but can I connect with you in an hour?"

What they say: "My child would never do something like that." This one comes from parents when they receive a call about their child's behavior.

- **What they mean:** It sounds like denial, but what it really reveals is anxiety and fear from someone who is facing a situation they'd never considered happening to them. It also means they are aligning with their child rather than the staff member(s) involved.
- **How to reply:** Again, addressing their feelings by responding to their intended meaning will alleviate the potential for a "he said, she said" argument. "I understand this is a surprise and out of character for your child. I plan to discuss it with your child to see if we can get to the root of the problem."

What they say: "My partner/spouse and I would like to meet with you." This often comes from a parent when they are upset and want a face-to-face conversation in which they can bring another parent along for a meeting—reinforcement, if you will. It means the parent needs it to be "two against one."

- **What they mean:** "I feel alone and need help navigating this situation." My sister openly admits to saying this to school staff. Her son has had challenges at school, and she is the primary contact when the school reaches out to her. When she goes to meetings, though, she feels she gets more respect and compromise when her husband is in the room. I think of her often when a parent tells me they're bringing someone else to a meeting, because I know they are trying to tell me they are worried they won't be seen, heard, or helped without it. It also might mean the parent needs help at home and wants the other parent to understand, firsthand, what the school's perspective might be.

- **How to reply:** I used to feel threatened and outnumbered when this happened, but I now consider this a sign that I need to do everything possible to lead a fully collaborative meeting. "Absolutely. Please bring whomever you'd like to the meeting. The more ideas we have in the room, the better!" If this makes you feel anxious about being outnumbered, you can always invite some other experts to join you in the meeting—a teacher, guidance counselor, an assistant principal. Again, this shouldn't be seen as reinforcement of "sides" but as a way to increase perspectives and potential solutions.

There are many other examples of people saying things when they mean something else, requiring the listener to pause and make sure they're answering the right question. Not long ago, I worked with a teacher who was furious that she was held financially responsible for some technology that had been ruined under her watch. She'd taken the device home to work on it, and one of her children, thinking it was a toy, played with it and dropped it in a sink full of water. She ranted about the injustice of being charged for the equipment when she'd been planning to work on it after school hours. I let her vent, and as I listened, it occurred to me that she wasn't mad about the $300 replacement. She was upset because she was struggling with several other things. The hardware hadn't been working in her classroom, and she didn't have time to figure it out during the school day; her students were not meeting behavioral expectations in the classroom; she was working hard and never felt caught up. I told her it was normal to struggle with those issues, and together we brainstormed solutions to alleviate her stress. I had a technology coach come help her implement the new equipment, we set some timelines so she didn't have to feel so pressed for outcomes so quickly, and she relaxed into the process rather than focusing on the end game. I was glad I'd listened to what she was saying—and what she really meant with her words.

When Conflict Becomes Combative

As stated earlier, people only battle in one direction. They compromise in both. If someone is battling, they can't give up their stance. They are stubborn, unwilling to bend, certain that they are right and others are wrong. They see a situation only in terms of "sides"—their side and that of the enemy. These are the times conflict will become aggressive and combative. In my experience, the only way through is to pause, wait, and strategize. If the situation has become damaging to others, especially students, it might be time for a forced compromise—a mandate, perhaps, or an ultimatum. "This behavior cannot continue any longer. We need changes to occur starting today. Let's think about what can be done to ensure a positive outcome." Moving someone out of the situation, insisting on respectful or professional behavior norms, or finding a way to start over might all be steps to consider.

It's Our Job

The very first school principals—"principal teachers," as they were called—were responsible for overseeing teachers and managing discipline—in other words, for managing conflicts. Since then, principals' jobs have gotten exceedingly more complex, but this basic premise still holds. It is our job to manage conflict. As I have mentioned multiple times in this book, we can't avoid conflict; it is here, it will keep coming, and we are paid to manage it. Following a healthy process—to *anticipate* it, *analyze* it, and *act* to resolve it—makes our jobs infinitely easier. Rather than resent conflict, accepting that its management is what we are paid to do brings acceptance and peace.

Be Part of the Work

I have a friend who leads literacy instruction for her district. Despite many opportunities to move into full-time consulting, she has retained her position as a teacher and does residual consulting work in the summer. I once asked her why she hadn't left teaching; after all, it would be much more lucrative financially and would utilize her massive amount of expertise in literacy. "Well, I just feel like I need to be in the muck with the teachers," she said. "I can't stand up and talk about the best way to teach students to read unless I am doing it." The importance of this approach applies to leadership. If I don't model and lead conflict management, I can't ask others to do it. I need to be patient, empathetic, kind, clear, fair, and thorough in my own behaviors related to conflict, and I need to articulate the importance of these behaviors in others.

Ask for Help

With that said, we shouldn't be in the muck as the lone leader. It's important to ask for help when needed. The emotional toll of managing conflict can easily overwhelm a principal, and there are times that situations get so complicated they need an outside lens. As an example, years ago, I relied on input from colleagues to handle a tricky situation. One of my paraprofessionals asked to meet with me. She shared some concerns about a teacher, making a faint suggestion about inappropriate behavior. It wasn't an accusation, exactly, but the potential allegations were extremely serious. The paraprofessional was so careful and vague with her words, I didn't know if the two were just having a disagreement or if the paraprofessional had truly witnessed the teacher crossing professional and ethical lines. I picked up the phone and called our Human Resources department and shared the exact words that were shared with me. Because what she'd said was so vague, and because there were exactly zero other indications of a problem—from myself, from teachers, from students—we did not launch an investigation. I knew I was legally on solid ground, but I still felt uncertain about how to proceed. I called a few members of my network to get their perspective. They all agreed I couldn't pursue an investigation based on nebulous information and gave me some tips about how to observe and monitor the situation. With help from professional friends, I felt reassured and able to develop a plan. Interestingly, the paraprofessional left my building at the end of that school year. She took a job in a neighboring district, where she made similar suggestions about one of the teachers there. When her accusations were investigated, it grew into a local news story. Although those allegations were debunked, it was damaging for the entire school community. To this day, I'm glad I didn't work alone; colleagues helped me think clearly and appropriately.

Feelings Aren't Facts

One of the challenges of being a principal is how often others get angry with us, even when we are trying to do good by them, even when we are advocating for them, even when we make decisions that will help them in the end. It makes me think of a friend of mine, whom I'll call Ami. Not long ago, she told me about a pivotal moment she'd had after a terrible fight with her teenage daughter. They stood in her kitchen, staring at each other, seething, furious, a showdown of wills. Ami was spiraling: She felt like a failure as a mother; her daughter was unkind, lacked empathy, and had no regard for authority; she was probably going to move out and never come home again; the world was ending. But then, after a long silence, her daughter said, "Mom. Just because I'm angry at you doesn't mean you did anything wrong." It was an olive branch, but it was also an important lesson in conflict management. It's true for students, but we forget that it's true of adults too. Just like a parent sometimes makes their child angry by doing what is right for them, there are times our students, staff, or community is mad at us, but it doesn't mean we did anything wrong. In fact, we might be doing something right.

Professional Love Language

When working with adults in conflict, I try to prioritize my relationship with the person struggling, to make them feel comfortable and valued. I do this by taking a swing at identifying their professional love language. Many of us are familiar with Gary Chapman's work with five love languages in relationships (2019). Chapman also teamed up with Paul White to write about appreciation languages at work. My "conflict management version" of Chapman and White's work is to know how to connect with someone, disarm their defenses, and open the door to a conversation. As an example, some people need to know they are appreciated. Others need heartfelt compliments after a job well done. Others need to be respected and treated as if their input and opinion are valued.

Still others need time and space to be alone. Many people—myself included—need to know that others can see how hard they are working and recognize their effort. A simple acknowledgment of workload—"I know you're carrying a lot, and your work ethic has allowed our school to do great things"—does wonders for morale and can take a situation of high conflict into one of calm productivity.

Lead Around

I worked with a principal recently who was struggling with an ongoing conflict with a teacher. No matter what the principal did, she was met with silent, resistant behavior. The teacher had virtually stopped speaking to the principal, looking down during staff meetings or ducking out of the hallway when the two were likely to pass one another. At evaluation time, the teacher refused to even read her written evaluation, much less sign it. No other teacher on the staff had an issue with the principal, but this teacher seemed intent on making one.

"What should I do?" the principal asked. "I want to bridge the problem between us, but she won't even look at me."

"Lead around," I said, passing on advice I'd been given from a friend when I had been in a similar situation. "Keep doing what you always do. Stay in compliance with evaluation dates. In the classroom, hold her to the same standard you hold other teachers. If she is insubordinate, follow your HR department's guidelines for addressing it. Don't seek a confrontation, but don't ignore her behavior, either." Leading around resistance will show the rest of the school community that you won't be deterred by the behavior of one person.

Final Thoughts and Favorite Moments

I love looking back on journals, but I rarely have the discipline to write every day. I found a way to both accomplish daily writing and have fun doing it. Just this year, I started a new approach: a "favorite moment of the day" journal. Each day as I leave work, I jot down a three- or four-sentence summary of a moment that made me feel accomplished, happy, amused, or satisfied with my work. Looking back at entries, I have begun to see a trend: my very favorite moments of the day almost always circle around a problem that was solved. A child who overcomes a problem with a friend and summarizes it into a snappy, sweet remark; a parent who feels heard and calmed; a teacher who is valued and vindicated. These entries help me recognize how much I enjoy guiding others through conflict. This doesn't mean you need a journal. It means you might be someone who gets joy from conflict resolution. If so, you're likely doing a great job—and doing the right job.

References

American School Counselor Association (ASCA). (n.d.). *School counselor roles & ratios*. Schoolcounselor.org. https://www.schoolcounselor.org/About-School-Counseling/School-Counselor-Roles-Ratios

Chapman, G., & White, P. (2019). *The 5 languages of appreciation in the workplace: Empowering organizations by encouraging people.* Moody Publishers.

Justia Law. (n.d.). *Goss v. Lopez*, 419 U.S. 565 (1975). https://supreme.justia.com/cases/federal/us/419/565/

Hansen, M., & Quintero, D. (2022, March 9). Scrutinizing equal pay for equal work among teachers. Brookings.edu. https://www.brookings.edu/research/scrutinizing-equal-pay-for-equal-work-among-teachers/

Merod, A. (2023, January 11). Seattle Public Schools sues social media companies Amid Youth Mental Health Crisis. *K-12 Dive.* https://www.k12dive.com/news/seattle-schools-sues-social-media-mental-health/640159

National Center for Education Statistics (NCES). (n.d.). Elsi: Elementary and secondary information system. https://nces.ed.gov/ccd/elsi/

U.S. Bureau of Labor Statistics. (2022, September 8). *Social workers: Occupational outlook handbook.* https://www.bls.gov/ooh/community-and-social-service/social-workers.htm

Index

The letter *f* following a page locator denotes a figure.

About the Author

Jen Schwanke, EdD, is a longtime educator who has taught or led at all levels. She is the author of three previous books: *You're the Principal! Now What? Strategies and Solutions for New School Leaders, The Principal Reboot: 8 Ways to Revitalize Your School Leadership,* and *The Teacher's Principal: How School Leaders Can Support and Motivate Their Teachers.* She has written for *EL Magazine, Choice Literacy, Education Week Teacher, Principal,* and *Principal Navigator.* Dr. Schwanke is a cohost of the popular "Principal Matters" podcast and has presented at conferences for ASCD, NAESP, Battelle for Kids, RRCNA, and various state and local education organizations. She has provided professional development to various districts in the areas of school climate, personnel, and instructional leadership. An adjunct graduate instructor in educational administration, Dr. Schwanke currently serves as a deputy superintendent in Ohio.

Related ASCD Resources

At the time of publication, the following resources were available (ASCD stock numbers in parentheses).

Compassionate Coaching: How to Help Educators Navigate Barriers to Professional Growth by Kathy Perret and Kenny McKee (#121017)

CRAFT Conversations for Teacher Growth: How to Build Bridges and Cultivate Expertise by Sally J. Zepeda, Lakesha Robinson Goff, and Stefanie W. Steele (#120001)

Forces of Influence: How Educators Can Leverage Relationships to Improve Practice by Fred Ende and Meghan Everette (#120009)

From Underestimated to Unstoppable: 8 Archetypes for Driving Change in the Classroom and Beyond by Ashley Lamb-Sinclair (#123017)

The Principal as Chief Empathy Officer: Creating a Culture Where Everyone Grows by Thomas R. Hoerr (#122030)

The Principal Reboot: 8 Ways to Revitalize Your School Leadership by Jen Schwanke (#121005)

Small Shifts, Meaningful Improvement: Collective Leadership Strategies for Schools and Districts by P. Ann Byrd, Alesha Daughtrey, Jonathan Eckert, and Lori Nazareno (#123007)

Teacher Observation and Feedback (Quick Reference Guide for Leaders) by Jen Schwanke (#QRG123047)

The Teacher's Principal: How School Leaders Can Support and Motivate Their Teachers by Jen Schwanke (#122035)

You're the Principal! Now What? Strategies and Solutions for New School Leaders by Jen Schwanke (#117003)

For up-to-date information about ASCD resources, go to www.ascd.org. You can search the complete archives of *Educational Leadership* at www.ascd.org/el. To contact us, send an email to member@ascd.org or call 1-800-933-2723 or 703-578-9600.

ascd whole child

The ASCD Whole Child approach is an effort to transition from a focus on narrowly defined academic achievement to one that promotes the long-term development and success of all children. Through this approach, ASCD supports educators, families, community members, and policymakers as they move from a vision about educating the whole child to sustainable, collaborative actions.

The Principal's Guide to Conflict Management relates to the **safe** and **supported** tenets. *For more about the ASCD Whole Child approach, visit* **www.ascd.org/wholechild.**

WHOLE CHILD
TENETS

1 HEALTHY
Each student enters school healthy and learns about and practices a healthy lifestyle.

2 SAFE
Each student learns in an environment that is physically and emotionally safe for students and adults.

3 ENGAGED
Each student is actively engaged in learning and is connected to the school and broader community.

4 SUPPORTED
Each student has access to personalized learning and is supported by qualified, caring adults.

5 CHALLENGED
Each student is challenged academically and prepared for success in college or further study and for employment and participation in a global environment.